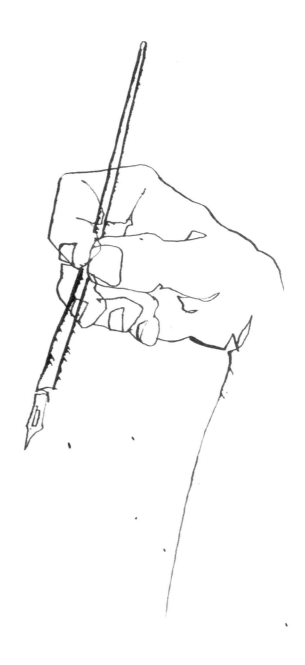

"In my time serving in Ukraine, I witnessed
the incredible strength and resourcefulness
of the Ukrainian people, which George Butler
so perfectly captures in his sensitive portraits
and profiles. This book is a powerful testament
to a people who are fighting for their lives and
country and, in doing so, are fighting for all
of us."
— William B. Taylor,
former US Ambassador to Ukraine

"George Butler is in the front rank of chroniclers
of our troubled times. His work shows the
power of paper and ink in the digital age."
— Jeremy Bowen, journalist

"George Butler reports from the frontline of
humanity producing images of astonishing
power. They stay in the mind for a long
time. Humane, compassionate, and deeply
thought-provoking."
— Stephen Fry, actor and author

"Reportage illustration at its finest."
— Ian Hislop, journalist and broadcaster

"George Butler's poignant illustrations show
what I see everyday in the soldiers and other
amputees recovering at the Superhumans
Center, that Ukrainians living and trying and
surviving is a powerful form of resistance."
— Olga Rudneva, CEO of Superhumans

To all the ordinary lives that find themselves in the middle of war.
And to Mum, Dad, Henry, and Gran for waiting at home.

☐ **Independence Monument wrapped in sandbags,** *Konstytutsii Square, Kharkiv, March 31, 2022*

UKRAINE
REMEMBER ALSO ME
TESTIMONIES FROM THE WAR

George Butler

CANDLEWICK STUDIO

an imprint of Candlewick Press

☐ **Odesa National Academic Opera and Ballet Theatre,** *Odesa, March 15, 2022*

CONTENTS

FOREWORD

As Ukraine's top diplomat in the United States of America, I am often asked: How, in the almost two years of war since Russia's all-out attack on your country, do you and other Ukrainians manage? Where do you find the strength to fight for your country, freedom, and democracy? How is Ukraine still standing?

George Butler's book *Ukraine: Remember Also Me* answers these questions. It presents memorable profiles and beautiful illustrations of ordinary Ukrainians who have risen to the challenge of war. Facing an invasion is a tragic and frightening experience. But the heroes of this book—Liza, Volodymyr, and Oleg—felt a responsibility to stand up and carry out their duty in defense of democracy, of their cities, of their sets of ideals. For others, like Dr. Yurii, Serhii, and Artem, it was a call to action. They chose not to abandon those in need but to work tirelessly to provide care. The uniting thread of all the stories collected in this book is the leitmotif of love. It shines through the powerful narrative, letting the reader appreciate Dima's love for his neighbors, Stanislav's love for his sons, Nata's love for her family. Love is the Ukrainian people's most powerful weapon.

The story of Ukraine is above all a story of its people. Ukraine is a young democracy, but with an ancient history. It is a nation that fought for independence, even during its darkest decades under Russian imperial rule. In 1991, the dream of independence came true, when, in the historic December 1 referendum, ninety-one percent of Ukrainians voted to break away from the Soviet empire. We became an independent country and we worked hard to perfect it—to have a government that is democratic, accountable, and ruled by its citizens.

Our democracy and independence have been constantly threatened by Russia, but in 2014, we faced the first great test of our existence. After the Revolution of Dignity, when Ukrainians once again proved their readiness to fight for their European and democratic future, Russia illegally annexed Crimea and occupied the East of our country. What saved us then? Our people. Having just thrown off a corrupt government dragging us back into the Russian orbit, back to oligarchic rule, Ukrainians went to the front in the hundreds of thousands to fight, to take care of the wounded, to feed those fighting. In those early days of the war, they alone saved Ukraine.

On February 24, 2022, we faced our ultimate test—Russia launched its unprovoked, full-scale invasion against its neighbor. The valor of our Armed Forces has captured the attention of the world; the daring offensives to liberate Bucha and Irpin, Kherson and Kharkiv have demonstrated that our brave defenders are capable of miracles on the battlefields. But, behind our great army are Ukraine's citizens, who complete their workday and then, in the other hours of their day, build drones, supply blood, raise funds, and provide care for veterans and the internally displaced.

George Butler's book tells the story of the citizen-side of this war, of football fans who once cheered together for their team and who now serve together on the front lines, of healthcare workers who refuse to leave behind those in need, of neighbors who save precious books and belongings from bombed-out apartments. George Butler captures these lives interrupted, and the determination of Ukrainians to endure until the ordinary good of their days can be restored. To endure until our country is whole again and until all our people return to their native land and live under peaceful skies.

Oksana Markarova,
Ambassador of Ukraine to the United States, February 2024

☐ **Destroyed Russian convoy,** *Vokzalna Street, Bucha, April 6, 2022*

INTRODUCTION

The title of this book was inspired by a poem by Taras Shevchenko (March 9, 1814–March 10, 1861), a poet of huge importance in the Ukrainian language and culture. Shevchenko's poem "My Testament," the last line of which is translated as "Remember also me," has startling significance when read today. Hidden among the headlines about this war runs a common theme: ordinary Ukrainians reacting to the Russian invasion in a bid to save themselves, their families, and their country. I hope this book will retain the honesty of their testimony and purity of their voices so that history can remember them also.

In February 2014, following the Maidan Revolution which ultimately ousted Ukrainian President Viktor Yanukovych, pro-Russian protests began in Donetsk and Luhansk. A month later Russia annexed the Crimean Peninsula and separatists took over Ukrainian government buildings, claiming Donetsk and Luhansk as republics under Russian control.

On April 6, 2014, Ukrainian forces responded by launching a military operation against the separatists in the east, who were supported by the Russian state.

In September 2014 a ceasefire was signed, which was subsequently broken and reinstated many times. Meanwhile both sides were dug into deep and often frozen trenches on the frontline, which hardly moved an inch.

On February 21, 2022, Russian President Vladimir Putin recognized Donetsk People's Republic (DPR) and Luhansk People's Republic (LPR) as independent states. At the same time, Russian forces gathered at the Russian and Belarusian borders with Ukraine although Russian officials denied an invasion was imminent. The world watched and waited to see what would happen next. Many people didn't believe Russia would launch an attack at all, but on February 24 at 5 a.m. everything changed. Russian troops moved into Ukraine and the full-scale invasion began.

Putin described it as a "special military operation" to protect the ethnic Russians in the east of Ukraine. Using words like "denazify" and "demilitarise" he claimed the invasion of another nation state was justified. The invasion was condemned by the United Nations and the International Court of Justice and heavy sanctions were imposed on Russia by Europe and the U.S.

It was assumed by many that Russia would take the capital city of Kyiv unchallenged, but Ukrainians had a different idea, and since then war has raged in Ukraine with horrific consequences to both sides.

Ukraine has a population of 43 million. Over ten thousand civilians have been killed in Ukraine since the invasion began. A further 3.7 million have been internally displaced, 6.3 million Ukrainian refugees globally. In this book I'd like to introduce you to a few Ukrainians who told me their stories.

Before February 24, 2022 the chances of you ever hearing about these people or even knowing their names were next to nothing. However, the events of the last two years have propelled them into the history books. Some of their stories may not have been sensational enough for the front pages, but they describe a common experience of war.

These characters are witnesses to heartbreak, unity, resolve, love, and destruction across Ukraine, during a time we might look back on as one of the most significant periods of the 21st Century. However the themes are not specific to Ukraine. They are familiar to many others at war. We imagine that if only the horrors could be documented as they happened in all their atrocious and vivid detail then perhaps, just perhaps, the cycle could be broken. Sadly, that is not yet the case. These are experiences shared by others I have met in Gaza and Syria, Yemen and Myanmar. And a reminder of the cyclical nature of wartime atrocity.

The drawings in this book were collected in March 2022, and March–April 2023 during my visits to Kyiv, Kharkiv, Izium, Bucha, Odesa, Kramatorsk, Poltava, and Sloviansk. The words that accompany them cover a century of history that has shaped the people and the borders of Ukraine. These are the subjects' own personal testimonies from interviews conducted as I sat and drew them. Sometimes they have been edited for clarity, or cross-checked with other accounts for balance. All of the people featured chose to be named.

It's not hard, even now, to find moments of positivity in Ukraine, but every person I met, almost without exception, had a harrowing story to tell. This is not meant to be a book of misery. I found such closeness, pride, defiance, community, identity, and strength in the vulnerable moments they shared with me. Their stories were brutal and sad, but they weren't desperate. There was and still is great hope and that shone through.

There have been many comparisons between World War II and this war: the noise of the artillery, young men believing they were only going away for training, the tape on the arms of soldiers identifying which side they are on, tank tracks ripping up tarmac roads, trenches cut deep into frozen earth with small spades, and the disruption to world order. They are easy comparisons to make and are what we think war looks like. But under the surface, I found much more. I found these stories revealed individual truths. They are authentic and raw—certainly unpolished in comparison to the tactical accounts on the front pages. I hope they are remembered and don't get lost in the white noise of modern warfare.

George Butler, February 2024

MY TESTAMENT

By Taras Shevchenko
Translated by John Weir

When I am dead, bury me
In my beloved Ukraine,
My tomb upon a grave mound high
Amid the spreading plain,
So that the fields, the boundless steppes,
The Dnieper's plunging shore
My eyes could see, my ears could hear
The mighty river roar.

When from Ukraine the Dnieper bears
Into the deep blue sea
The blood of foes . . . then will I leave
These hills and fertile fields—
I'll leave them all and fly away
To the abode of God,
And then I'll pray . . . . But till that day
I nothing know of God.

Oh bury me, then rise ye up
And break your heavy chains
And water with the tyrants' blood
The freedom you have gained.
And in the great new family,
The family of the free,
With softly spoken, kindly word
Remember also me.

December 25, 1845 in Pereyaslav

Reproduced with kind permission from the Shevchenko Museum, Toronto, Canada (www.shevchenko.ca)

MAP OF UKRAINE

Drawn Spring 2023

KEY

Russian-controlled territory before February 24, 2022

Russian-controlled territory since February 24, 2022

Territory regained by Ukrainian military forces

BELARUS

CHORNOBYL

ZHYTOMYR

LVIV

UKRA

MOLDOVA

WESTERN EUROPE

RUSSIA

BELARUS

UKRAINE

MOLDOVA

IZMAIL

MADAME OLGA, 99

Matriarch, great grandmother

KYIV

MADAME OLGA WAS BORN IN 1923. World War I was still a recent memory and World War II was sixteen years away. The Russian Revolution in 1917 had led to the collapse of the Russian Empire and the declaration of independence by Ukraine.

I met her 99 years later in her fourth floor apartment in Kyiv with her daughter, Valentyna. It was a small, top floor apartment, the interiors of which looked as though they hadn't changed for 40 years. We met there despite the continuing air raids in Kyiv because Olga was too frail to get down the stairs to a shelter. She was too frail to get out of bed at all.

I went into her room, where she lay with her Bible half-tucked under her pillow. The tiny shape of her body was only just visible under the thick blankets. Leaning against a huge pile of pillows, she propped herself up on her elbows and looked at me steadily. I saw her bird-like body, heard her wavering voice, and recognised her determined mind.

At first Olga was worried that I had come to take her away from her home and perhaps even her beloved country, so Mila, the volunteer aid worker who had introduced us, crouched, held both Olga's hands and positioned herself six inches from her face. She spoke loudly and reassuringly so Olga could hear and explained who I was and why I was there. It wasn't long before Olga took control of the situation, saying, "If you all stop asking questions I will tell you from the beginning." We did as we were told and she began her story, starting one hundred years before.

Madame Olga tells her story . . .

What can I tell you? I'm already 99 years old . . . I only remember those early parts of my life, Stalin's famine, World War II, and so on in tiny fragments. It was so horrible. And there's no one left from that time now—no one, just me.

I was born in 1923. I'm from Zhytomyr Oblast, Radomyshl' Raion, Mala Racha village. In 1935 my father had to join a collective farm. He was very much against it and didn't want to join, because he felt a lot of people in the farm were lazy. They didn't want to work. There were two collective farms in our village. One named after Voroshylov, which was poor, and another named after Molotov, which was better. There were some hard-working and wealthy people at Molotov and my father eventually agreed to go there. So, he joined, and we started to work. We were sent to work in the fields, to pull weeds out of the wheat fields. There were a lot of weeds. I worked as well. I was twelve years old then.

"Huge trouble has come to us."

[Olga goes on to talk about being a prisoner of war in Germany. The memory is clearly upsetting. She tells me she has forgotten the words to describe her feelings. In her agitation she mistakes Putin for Hitler, imagining it is the Germans who are invading again.]

God forbid this. Ukraine must stand. This is big trouble. It's horrifying. We must do our best to defend ourselves. Huge trouble has come to us.

When the war started [World War II], an order was issued to send a certain number of girls from our village, forcing them to work in Germany.

But I had a great pain in my leg, it was a heel abscess. My dad carried me out in his arms and put me in a cart. I was taken to Radomyshl', where a doctor examined my foot and said that it will be healed before we arrive in Germany. So, we were taken to Germany. I didn't know what the city was. They sent us for a bath. Then a group of us girls were taken by someone. . . . We went by the railroad. Dresden . . . Freital . . . Rabenau. Lübau is the name of the village we ended up in. I was in Germany from 1942 to 1945.

I can't remember the name of the people who took me. They always called him "Gerd herr" [indistinguishable]. His wife was Hilda. They lived with their mother. When the owner and his wife had a baby daughter, I had to babysit her, too.

The people there didn't seem bad at first. But then something happened—the owner's wife got something into her head and she started behaving strangely. She got worms, big ones . . . and she fed us those worms. They were thick as fingers.

One day we had enough. We ran away. It was autumn and cold. Me, my friend Olia Lopatiuk, and one guy climbed out of the window and ran away. We thought it would be better to find work in a factory. We took a train. My companions knew the way to go. We ended up in Dresden. There, we were spotted and taken to the police. Oh my God, I was so upset. The police questioned us and there was a person who translated. I told the truth about how our owner's wife was feeding us worms. They asked for the address, then the owner came, and he took us back to the village.

[After World War II was over, the area where Olga was living in Germany fell under Soviet control and the Soviet soldiers soon arrived. Initially Olga and her companions began to walk home, but the Soviet soldiers told her and two of her Ukrainian companions to herd 130 cows. Olga found the work extremely hard.]

"She got worms . . . she fed us those worms."

So at the end of the war we were conquered by our troops. They were Russians. Nobody organized the people. We all went back to ourselves, each to his own and decided to leave. We went to Dresden. We were three girls—me, Mariia from Dnipropetrovsk, and Olia Lopatiuk from Prypiat.

When we got to Dresden, we walked out of the train station and saw a cart. In it was a group of guys. One of them shouted, "Look, there are our girls there!" Because we were all young and he was a Slavic refugee like us, who could spot another Slavic refugee. Then we were all signed up to drive 130 cattle to Vinnytsia. The Soviet troops made us drive the cows all the way to Vinnytsia!

□ **Lines before curfew at the EKO Market,** *Kyiv, March 21, 2022*

That Slavic man [became] my husband: Yevtushenko Petro Petrovych. He is dead now. But he was from Obukhiv, Kyiv Oblast, and that was when I met him. I was 22 years old then. He was fourteen years older than me. And together we drove 130 cattle to Vinnytsia. At first we arrived at Proskurov, I think it was just inside Poland, because we seemed to have crossed the border by then. And I said to Petro, "From here, you know, I go to Zhytomyr. And you can go wherever you want." I said, "I'm going to the station to ask when our train departs." But the cows caught some disease so we had to stay there together on the Oder river for a whole month, because the cows were in quarantine. So that's how Petro came into the picture!

[History doesn't relate if the cows ever arrived in Vinnytsia. Olga's story is muddled after nearly 100 years of life, but there's no stopping her.]

"Such are my travels, God forbid . . ."

Eventually they allowed us to leave and we caught a big train which was going to Zhytomyr. We heard some horror stories about Western Ukraine, and what had happened there. I don't know why. . . . That night passed quietly though and nobody bothered us.

We got to Zhytomyr, left the train at a station near a sewing factory. I had wanted to work at that factory before the war, and it's right next door. So, we went out of the station, and then we went to my village, Mala Racha. And life went on. Petro, he stuck with me, we soon got married . . . Ukraine back then was ghastly.

I have a son Anatolii, born in 1948, a son Petro, born in 195— I forget the exact date . . .

My grandchildren are adults already!

Such are my travels, God forbid . . .

☐ Internally displaced people waiting in
Kyiv railway station, *Kyiv, March 28, 2022*

PETRO, 70

Book gatherer, locksmith

KRAMATORSK

ON THE MORNING I MET PETRO, at 8.30 a.m., a Russian missile ripped into a residential building near our meeting place in the middle of Kramatorsk, just off Akademichna Street. By now, of course, this wasn't a surprise to any of the civilians left in Kramatorsk. Ever since Russian forces began their invasion of Donetsk in April 2014, and especially since Russian Tochka-U missiles hit the railway station on April 8, 2022, killing 63 people, people expected this sort of indiscriminate bombardment.

Around the "strike site" I saw a group of men dressed in green work-uniforms and high-vis vests, clearing the broken branches and rubble. A team of military personnel collected scraps of the missile—perhaps for evidence one day in the International Criminal Court—while others cut chipboard to fit into the places where windows used to be. Most of the windows of the surrounding buildings had been blown out. People talked quietly as they swept the glass from their balconies onto the street. A food tent had been set up near the playground. Everyone carried out their tasks without fuss, hysteria or visible anger, showing how normal this situation had become. For now, real emotion was set aside.

At the front of the missile-hit building, opposite her house, sat a lady in a hooded black jacket with a ripped shoulder. Soot covered parts of her face. In front of her was a neat pile of belongings that she had pulled from the debris. She guarded them. I walked round the corner and saw a scene that at first made no sense at all. Hundreds of books had landed in a small rose garden outside the apartment building, blown there by the blast. The books lay open, with pages dangling in the bushes. Amongst it all stood Petro, collecting the books, folding them carefully, and stacking them up in piles.

Petro tells his story . . .

I decided to come and see what had happened. Then I saw the books. These were not my books, it wasn't my apartment, but I was brought up so that if I see a loaf of bread on the ground, I'll take it and put it somewhere. It's the same with books. They are spiritual food. I think the owners of the apartment had used the books to barricade the window but as the hit was inside the building, it blew everything out.

I was born in this city. I grew up here and have lived here all my life. Now I'm old. I worked all my life as a locksmith for New Kramatorsk Machine Building Factory (NKMZ). The factory continued until March 2022 and then it closed. After a year we received some money from our directors, for which I'm really grateful. But we still didn't have any work.

Now I live in a dormitory with my wife. It isn't what I expected. We never had lots of money, but we have a place to live and we have an opportunity to help our son.

You know what motivates me to keep going? My son and his family, who are in Kharkiv now. They have a daughter, my granddaughter, who is one and a half years old. I thought to myself, I need to live, because if I don't, who will marry her off? I need to live for a minimum of twenty years, even though I haven't seen her since the start of the full-scale war.

"It's the same with books. They are spiritual food."

☐ **Petro collecting books after a missile strike,** *Kramatorsk, March 14, 2023*

□ **Missile strike,** *near Akademichna Street, Kramatorsk, March 14, 2023*

YURII, 86

Widower, retired steelworker

MARIUPOL

I'VE NEVER MET A PERSON MORE DELIGHTED to be in a nursing home than Yurii, but once I heard the story of how he came to be there, I understood why. As other residents screamed and shouted around him, Yurii sat peacefully in this Kyiv surburb, eating a marshmallow biscuit, eloquently adding to my understanding of Mariupol.

Yurii was born in 1938, one year before the beginning of World War II. In 1939 Russia annexed Western Ukraine, which at the time was part of Poland, under the terms of the Nazi-Soviet Pact. During World War II it is estimated that 900,000 Ukrainian Jews were killed by the Nazis, as well as between five and seven million Ukrainians killed in battle. At the end of the interview I asked Yurii whether there were any similarities between World War II and this invasion. He said, "This is a brother-killing war. A war where Russian-speaking people kill Russian-speaking people."

Yurii tells his story . . .

I was born on March 31, 1938, in Dnipro. In 1941 my father, who was a coal miner, went to the Ural Mountains to work and he took me, my mom, and my elder brother with him. It wasn't a usual mine, it was full of Ukrainians and Crimean Tatars who had been deported from Crimea by Stalin. In 1944 all of my family had to move again to a different coal mine in Kazakhstan. Most of the people there spoke Kazakh and I didn't understand a single word!

A year later my father was sent to Dnipro to work at a mining institute, and I, age seven, was entered into the first creative school in Dnipro. Dnipro was in ruins as a result of the war and when we went to school we had to take wood from home to put in the stoves—to warm it up a bit. We could still see the dead bodies of German soldiers lying in the ruins. When I was fifteen my mother died—her health was affected by those years in the war and life in the Urals and in Kazakhstan.

In 1960 my father wanted me to go to Kramatorsk, where my elder brother was already working as an engineer. He was going to take care of me, but I didn't want to be taken care of so I ran away to Mariupol.

Mariupol was small at the time. It had about 30,000 residents who lived in small two-story, cottage-like buildings. I lived and worked there for 62 years, until the large-scale invasion in February 2022. I did well at work and at one point I had 2,000 people working under my direction. I watched how Mariupol grew over the years and saw all those nine-story buildings go up around me as more and more people came to work in different industries.

In 1972 I married my wife and we were given a spacious apartment in Mariupol. We had no children, but we had a happy life. We travelled a lot and I took her on expeditions to North Russia. We experienced a lot together. When she died in 2020 I was very lonely in our three-room apartment, but I still had our cat to keep me company.

The Russians invaded the city on February 25 and there was heavy fighting. I used to lie on the floor of my apartment . . . because that is what we'd been told to do. Then on February 26 a bomb hit the house. My arms were burned. Two younger guys pulled me out and I was taken to a building where there were some wounded Russian soldiers and wounded civilians. On the roof of the nine-story building where I was taken there were machine guns and they were shooting all around the city.

The cat died in the explosion . . . and I lost all my possessions, all my library of 2,600 books, and all my collection of postmarks. When my two saviors rescued me from my house, I only had my passport, my factory ID card, and 40 Ukrainian hryvnias in my pockets.

Later I was taken to the clinic at the Azovstal steelworks, where they kept me for a month and a half. In the first two days the Russians checked my documents, but they soon realized that I was old already and they left me alone.

Once a day, the Russians gave me a glass of hot water, with spaghetti and potatoes in it. Just imagine. . . I lost over 90 pounds during that time. The Russians treated us like cattle and they looted whatever they could around Mariupol.

I could see from the windows how the city I had watched being built was being destroyed. I could hear the sounds of fighting. The Russians wanted to create a positive picture of what was happening and one day I saw a cook from the kitchen with some soldiers, with a bowl of food, being filmed. They wanted it to look like they were liberating the Ukrainians.

Eventually some of my acquaintances from the factory [where I worked] found me . . . somehow . . . and paid the Russians to release me. By that time I was so weak that I had to be helped to walk down from the seventh floor to the ground floor. As they were helping me down the stairs of the clinic, one of the Russian soldiers asked my age. When I said I was 85, he said, "Throw him away. It's time for him to die, not walk around."

In May I was helped by a Jewish organization to leave Mariupol to make my way to Dnipro, which was originally my hometown.

One of my junior colleagues at the factory where I worked, called Anatolii, also left Mariupol and came to near Dnipro. Since I was alone, he, his wife, and his son decided that they would take care of me. This is how I ended up in here, in this home in Kyiv. I am still smiling and I am hoping that one day Mariupol will be liberated and that I will at least be able to visit the tomb of my wife and my mother.

"... a bomb hit the house. My arms were burned."

☐ **A makeshift bridge under the destroyed Irpin Bridge,** *Irpin, near Kyiv, April 2, 2022*

YARA, 27

Combat medic, drone pilot, mother

SLOVIANSK

TOURNIQUETS, A DRONE, SOME GRENADES, a modified Kalashnikov and an old 4x4 are the tools of Yara's trade. It's a trade she has been perfecting since 2020, when she joined the Marine Corps of the Ukrainian Armed Forces.

Yara is a combat medic, a drone pilot, an English literature graduate, and a mother to Orisa, age eight. She drives a truck called the Gipsy King, named partly after the well-known band she loves so much, but also because she and her team have spent so long living in it, they feel like "gypsies of war".

At first I struggled to get a sense of who she was. Where did the poetry fit with the decorated ammunition cases and her striking shoulder-length braids? But, as she began to talk and told me her story, it all started to make sense.

In the back of the Gipsy King, which doubles up as an ambulance transporting people from the frontline to the first aid stations, first aid kits hung next to her armored vest with ammunition cases. A SpongeBob SquarePants teddy was pinned to the wall. She carried two bags. In one was her combat medic equipment, with vials of liquid painkiller and other life-saving equipment, and in the other was a drone. This drone was available to buy on the civilian market but it had a small velcro holder attached underneath. A tiny finned grenade fitted into the holder, with a screw-in detonator, which Yara assured me over a cup of coffee wouldn't go off while I drew her. These drones have become an important part of the fight against Russian forces in the east of Ukraine.

Interviewed March 17, 2023

Yara tells her story . . .

Until 2022 I was a volunteer paramedic in the Hospitallers, and before that I was studying for my MA in English Literature. Then in 2022, before the full-scale invasion was underway from February, I signed up with the Ukrainian armed forces. My husband [Peter] is serving in the same company as I am. He used to be in 10th Brigade and I was in the Marine Corps. However, during the full-scale invasion he came to Luhansk, to where we were fighting, and the commander gave him permission to serve with us . . . and to man a machine gun. It meant that at any time we could have witnessed the death of the other. But so far we have been lucky. There have been many opportunities for either of us to be killed. One such time was in a village 30 miles north of Mariupol, where we fought some very fierce and difficult battles in March 2022. The Russians were trying to break though there but we were resisting their attacks. We took very many casualties in the fighting.

I remember there was a column of Russian tanks, and they were coming towards our observation post. There were five of us there, including me and my husband. We had an APC [Armored Personnel Carrier] as well. We had been told that this column was made up of Ukrainians who were trying to escape Mariupol, but I put a drone in the air and I saw that they were Russians.

Our commander took my husband and went to double check, just in case we were mistaken. The lead tank in the column saw them and pointed their gun towards them. Then, by chance, they saw the APC and decided to aim at the APC first, which they did. They destroyed it. I was very near the APC when it exploded. We had just enough time, with all the shooting going on around us, to make it back to the forest line. And we were alive! It was March 5—I even remember the date. After that we went to the village and by combining forces with another company, we managed to stop this Russian column. It was fourteen trucks in total. After that we spent seven days defending Zachativka village. They attacked the village from three different approach

" . . . at any time we could have witnessed the death of the other."

roads, so we shot everything we had at them. One day, I had three soldiers wounded within five minutes of each other, one after the other. We lost so many people, including my platoon commander senior lieutenant.

There are other women in my company, but the army doesn't encourage women to take up combat posts in the Marine Corps. If you want to fight in combat you have to take a difficult test. I wanted to fight very much, so I did the physical test and I passed. I earned their trust, and that is why they let me do this.

"There have been many opportunities for either of us to be killed."

MARIIA, 76 & OLEKSANDR, 51

Mother & brother of Dima

BUCHA

BEFORE BUCHA BECAME A HEADLINE, it was a desirable place for the middle classes to live, just outside Kyiv. Now it is a place known for a list of barbaric atrocities committed on a civilian population by the Russian army since February 27, 2022. It is the place that confirmed what many Ukrainians feared was happening in towns the Russians had captured. The discoveries in those few days after its liberation led to as many questions as they answered. Questions about the war, Vladimir Putin, and the human condition. Could it really be true? Were the soldiers ordered to carry out these acts? How could one person do that to another? Surely the young Russian soldiers didn't know what they were doing? Does the Russian public know what its soldiers are doing?

One year later Mariia and Oleksandr were still trying to make sense of what happened and answer these questions.

Mariia was born in 1950, six years after Joseph Stalin deported an estimated 400,000 Crimean Tatars to Siberia, and four years before Nikita Khrushchev gave the Crimean Peninsula to Ukraine.

In 1972, at the height of the Soviet Union, she gave birth to her son Oleksandr, then her son Serhii. She moved to Bucha in 1980, where her third son Dmytro (Dima) was born in 1982.

I spoke to Mariia and Oleksandr about her son and his brother, Dima, who was killed on their doorstep in Bucha almost exactly a year earlier. We were joined briefly by Serhii. Amidst their grief they shone a light on what life was like under Russian occupation during that fateful period.

Mariia and Oleksandr tell their story . . .

MARIIA – As we woke at 5 a.m. [on February 24], we heard bombing. We turned on the radio and TV and could not believe that the war had begun. I couldn't believe that it had really happened because my husband was Russian and I have many relatives there. I couldn't believe that Russia would attack us.

OLEKSANDR – Our relatives from Russia often used to come and visit us. And after the war began, they said, "Don't worry, we will just kill the Nazis and that is all that will happen!"

Everybody stayed in the apartment on the 24th, 25th, 26th. We could hear the battle in Hostomel Airport. The neighbors went down to the basement but we didn't move there because we live on the first floor. I suggested to my mom that she should leave, but she said, "Where would we go? We have cats!"

"Where would we go?"

On February 27 the Russians arrived. Many people escaped to Kyiv and ran with their bags and their children. By March 3 the Russians were everywhere. People were still escaping to Kyiv though—but the Russians started to stop them, and began to kill them. They started shooting everyone they saw . . . shooting cars, shooting people.

MARIIA – I saw people in three civilian cars shot by Russian soldiers.

OLEKSANDR – My brother Dima had a workshop in the basement where he worked as a freelance electrician. He was always down there. On March 3, Dima helped the people who were escaping from Hostomel and downtown Bucha to hide in his workshop in the basement. He gave them towels and things.

MARIIA – There were between 25 and 28 people in the basement, and 8 or 9 children with them.

OLEKSANDR – Dima was killed on March 4. He was standing at the corner of the building with his neighbor Vlad, watching what was happening. They saw the Russian soldiers kill some people behind the Fora [the supermarket on Yablunska Street]. People began to run to hide in the basement. Vlad, who was fifteen or sixteen, started running first. He said to Dima, "Run with me," and Dima replied,

"I have never run from anyone in my life." The soldiers came from behind the building and Vlad ran down to the basement. But Dima didn't. Dima sat on the stairs to the basement . . . and began to smoke . . .

Two soldiers came towards the basement and saw Dima. They saw that he was not a soldier and that he was a civilian and they shot him, with three individual shots. One of them went to Dima after they had shot him and checked that he was dead. Dima's soul was kind but he had a sharp tongue.

I was told all this by a neighbor who was hiding in the basement. I told my mother the next day—on March 5 in the morning.

MARIIA – When I was told I fell down and Oleksandr caught me. Dima was 41 years old. He wasn't married but he had built his own house nearby and he had a girlfriend. She has left the country.

OLEKSANDR – All day long on March 5 I was worried about Mariia, my mother, and I didn't let her see Dima. She wanted to take Dima to our apartment to wash him and change his clothes.

All this time he was lying outside on the stairs. There was an unofficial curfew, so the street was empty and everybody was frightened to go outside. Russian soldiers were killing people all the time. It was enough to walk around the street for them to kill you. There were no Ukrainian soldiers here at the time—just civilians.

MARIIA – I saw eleven civilians killed through these two windows.

SERHII – They even shot at anyone who was looking out of the windows, like we were cats and dogs. The soldiers were drunk and they were walking around and if they noticed any movement they began to shoot.

OLEKSANDR – Eventually, Mariia went outside to Dima on the stairs, to wash him and change his clothes. She wanted to take Dima to our apartment, but the people who were in the basement said to her, "Please do not do this . . . because Dima was protecting us when he was alive and also now when he is dead."

"I have never run from anyone in my life."

□ **Cement truck roadblock,** *Soborna Street, Bucha, April 6, 2022*

When the Russian soldiers came through they saw a dead person and they didn't go into the basement. That was how Dima's body protected the basement. The Russians just dropped grenades into the basement of the house a few doors away. That house had five children in it. The Russian soldiers came and knocked at the door of the basement. Nobody answered so they just dropped the grenade. That was house number 203G. This house is 203A.

MARIIA – Dima was a sacrifice and he protected them.

"Dima was a sacrifice ..."

OLEKSANDR – On March 6, in the evening, we took Dima just inside the apartment, behind the inside door. On March 7 the situation was calmer and many people from the basement went to Irpin. The only non-dangerous way to escape was by walking. It was very dangerous to leave by car or even by bicycle . . .

On March 7 Russian soldiers came to our apartment to check on us, and that morning we carried Dima's body to beside the house. We laid him on the ground and covered him with a towel.

MARIIA – First they asked Oleksandr to come out of the flat and then they called me outside too. Hearing Russian speech, I began to cry. A Russian soldier pointed his gun at me, so I went closer to him and he asked me, "Aren't you afraid of me?" I said, "Of course not. You're Ruski Mir [Russian term which means "Russian World"]. Why would I be afraid of you?"

OLEKSANDR – On March 8 the soldiers did another search of the apartment. They wanted to make sure that we weren't hiding any military. As they left I went out after them and asked if I could bury my brother. I didn't feel scared. They said, "OK. Yes, we will come back tomorrow and you can bury him."

I got a shovel, and we took Dima's body outside. The weather was like now. Actually it's March 8 today, so it is one year tomorrow. We dragged Dima's body to a place in the yard near the house. Russian soldiers walked beside us. One of them even helped Mariia to dig. Two of them watched. Mariia spoke to them but I refused to talk to them. Mariia told them we have relatives in Russia and one of them said, "You should evacuate to Russia." Then I looked into his eyes and said to him, "When you return home to Russia you will not recognise your country." I meant that there was no way back from the step that Russia had taken in this war. The soldier didn't reply.

The main thing was that we hadn't seen how Dima died. Some people recognised some of the soldiers who shot Dima. They asked one of them, "Why did you kill Dima? Why did you kill a man who was just sitting and smoking?" And he answered sarcastically, "Because he was wearing green trousers," which is the equivalent of just saying f*** off and leave me alone.

People began to survive. It became calmer and we cooked and made fires outside the apartments even while the Russians were still around. But we never went further away than the yard. Between us we don't own many shovels, so all the neighbors came to borrow our shovel so that they could bury their relatives. So many people are buried around here.

The last opportunity for people to escape was March 12, through the last corridor out of Bucha. After that it wasn't possible to leave. So, from March 12, we stayed here. We cooked and made food outside—it was cold. We had no electricity, no heating, no water until April 1, when the Russian soldiers finally left.

MARIIA – There was only one of the Russian soldiers who talked to the people here. He was a young man from Siberia, which is far from here. He answered our questions. He said that he hadn't known that they were coming to Ukraine, to the war, but he thought that they were going to military training. He seemed surprised.

But people asked him, "Did you see how many people you killed? This is not training." And he just didn't respond.

But the loss of my son Dima is like an open wound. Nobody knows what would be if they [the Russian soldiers] had come into the basement.

OLEKSANDR – Although we first buried Dima behind the house, the experts exhumed him later. On May 2, we buried him at the city cemetery. We think that we did everything right.

"So many people are buried around here."

☐ **Mass graves,** *St. Andrew's Church, Bucha, April 8, 2022*

DR. YURII

Doctor

IZIUM

OUTSIDE AN UNINVITING DOOR in an old hospital corridor, I sat and waited to speak to Dr. Yurii. The front of the hospital had been destroyed by a Russian missile on March 8, 2022.

It's easy to get a sense of a person from how prepared they are to speak with a journalist. Dr. Yurii was in no rush. Quite rightly, the line of patients waiting outside his door was attended to first. It showed what a dedicated character Dr. Yurii was and how he understood the priorities of his work.

Patients sat on mismatched chairs and benches, hoping they would not have to wait too long to see him. Izium had been heavily bombed when the Russians took the town in March 2022, and then again when it was "de-occupied" in September 2022, so there had been many civilian casualties for Dr. Yurii to treat.

At the end of the day, when I was allowed into his office, I found Dr. Yurii in blue doctor's scrubs in front of a yellow wall—the two colors that have branded every inch of recent Ukrainian life. Otherwise, the room was dark, the windows boarded up since the missile attack. He was hunched over his desk. He didn't look up very often, even as he talked, but when he did, I found myself drawing the face of a man who clearly cared far more about everyone around him than about himself. He was so concerned for other people, it was almost impossible to get him to talk about himself. That's why I never knew his age.

Dr. Yurii was convinced that his story was totally ordinary.

Dr. Yurii tells his story . . .

My story began on March 6, 2022, when I started living in the hospital. I got up that day, went to work and stayed there until September. Most of our patients also stayed in the hospital from March 6. Mostly they were lonely, elderly, or disabled. They were taken to the basement when the shelling started and stayed there. That's how our basement life began.

The evacuation of the city started in the evening of March 7. They took people to Sloviansk. In the morning of that day the bridges over the river were destroyed to prevent the Russian army from moving forward. The connection (phone and road) between our city and unoccupied Ukraine was broken. My family lived on the other side of the river. A couple of days later I decided to go there and see if they were alive, as I hadn't heard from them. The only other doctor in the hospital and I decided to go and see if our relatives were OK. If everything was OK, we agreed we would come back and continue to help people here in the hospital in the city, because there were lots of citizens still here. But I was the only one who came back. But I don't blame anybody.

> "I often say that our hospital is guarded by a guardian angel."

Before the full-scale war there were 500 medical staff in the hospital. Now we have about 200 people. I usually work till the last patient. I often say that our hospital is guarded by a guardian angel.

When the Russians occupied the city, we all lost a lot of weight, but after the de-occupation in September we all got fat again! It's much calmer now.

Once during the occupation, I spoke to a Russian soldier. He was swearing a lot, saying, "Izium is f*** difficult to hold." I told him to look at Izium's history. It has never been easy with Izium. Never. During all the wars that have happened here, we have always had huge human losses and heavy fighting. During World War II the city passed into different sides two or three times. It's difficult to pass us by.

This time about 80% of the city was destroyed, according to some experts. Now, Izium is the most mine-littered city in the Kharkiv region. Lately we have many people taken to the hospital after blowing up on a mine. Most of them are young people, who're roaming the woods in search of scrap metal on the positions where the Russians were based. Just today we had a patient who was walking in the woods and stepped on a PFM-1 mine. He lost his right foot. Almost each week we have a new "suffered from mines" casualty.

But the good thing is that Ukrainians recover very quickly. Have you seen the energy here in the hall? People are fighting for their place in the line.

I'm always telling everybody how everything that we managed to achieve under the occupation—how we kept going—wasn't possible without each member of our team contributing. Everyone helped—we divided the responsibilities and tried to be organized.

For example, in March 2022 we had a problem with the water. If you went out of the hospital it was very dangerous, as the Russians might see you and shoot you. So, when it snowed, we just collected the snow, melted it and used it for our needs.

I've never been a person who chases material well-being, but during this past year I became much less dependent on material values. You can have millions in money, but then you die, and nothing. Human life is the most precious thing. It has the biggest value.

Here's an example of what I mean. My neighbors came and said, "Oh. A missile has hit your house." Of course, I was worried. I wanted to go immediately and check if it was true. But I'm so busy in the hospital, I only managed to go home after a while. When I did go home, I saw that a part of my house was totally damaged. And I burst out laughing. My neighbors said, "Are you crazy, why are you laughing?" I told them, "I'm laughing because it's good that I work so much and haven't been home for a while. If I had been there, maybe I wouldn't be speaking with you now."

So, working day and night saved my life. I'm happy to be here now and able to speak with you!

"Human life is the most precious thing."

STANISLAV, 34 & VOLODYMYR, 7

Father & son

KHARKIV

ON THE FOURTH FLOOR OF THE KHARKIV CITY CLINICAL HOSPITAL I met Volodymyr, who was recovering in bed from two operations after a shooting at a checkpoint, which had lodged a bullet in his brain and killed his mother, Daria.

In this small room with two beds, Volodymyr was living with his father, Stanislav, and his brother, Viktor, who was three years old. Together they were trying to rebuild their lives from scratch, against all odds, with the person they all loved the most now missing. This was very moving to look in on. In the basement of the hospital, amongst the foundations and the heating system, Stanislav's brother was living with his wife so they could be close by, but safe from the nearby artillery in the north of the city.

When I met him a month after the shooting, Volodymyr was learning how to use his legs again. He had been in bed so long that the muscle wastage had made his body look disproportionally small compared to the size of his head. This was accentuated by the enormous bandage wrapped around his skull. It was attached with multi-colored animal bandages that seemed out of place alongside the story his father Stanislav was about to tell. Stanislav and I sat in an empty hospital ward room away from Viktor and Volodymyr while he told me about what happened to his son.

Interviewed March 29, 2022 & March 11, 2023 55

Stanislav tells Volodymyr's story . . .

It happened on February 28, near the church at the intersection that's not far from here. That day was maybe the hardest. Some rockets and bombs hit apartments and buildings in the area and . . . my wife was with my sons and my brother and his wife in our rented apartment.

On that day some windows were broken in our apartment, on the balcony, and almost all the windows of the nearest buildings. They began to panic and they decided that they should move to the apartment of my brother. My wife and two children went in one car and my brother and his wife in their car.

They drove for maybe 500 yards and the car with my wife and children was shot with an automatic gun by our soldiers. . . . I don't know why it happened but as a result she was killed directly. And my oldest son got this bullet in his head. And the youngest one got some scratches on his face.

Daria was 34, she was like an angel.

" . . . it's war and this kind of situation happens in war . . ."

[Like many conversations of this nature, this is accompanied by scrolling through old pictures. It's as if there is so much pain it's impossible for one person to manage, and if talking about it to a stranger might help disperse just a tiny bit of it, or bring back a positive memory for a moment, then that would be worth it. Stanislav shows me pictures of Daria at the beach by the Sea of Azov.]

We had a tradition made by her: every year on our wedding day we took a photo together. When we bought a car, we took a photo with the car; after that with one child; after that with the second child. I think we will stop the tradition now, it's enough.

[Stanislav shows me a photo of the car after the shooting.]

56

That was the car, it's the place where the incident happened. These are the points from bullets, one, two and three, four . . . five—two directly to the driver. And two in the back. Also you can see there are no windows at all—we don't know how many bullets went through the windows.

The Ukrainian army would like to write in the report that it was just a car accident. They also wrote that the cause of death was a broken neck. Only after we discussed it did they also write that it happened because of the war and some metal parts were found in her body. That is their position, it's war and this kind of situation happens in war . . . here . . . I don't know . . . each day?

They said that she didn't stop when they made an order for her to stop. But no one was there, no one was there! No one told her to stop . . . they just shoot . . .

We will see if Volodymyr will have another operation. I don't know how long we will be here. If you look at his head directly, the left part of his brain is swollen because the bullet has pushed the brain against the bones of the head . . . and it compressed, and now the surgeon looks each week at the results, and I hope that we won't need it but it may be that we need one more operation. I hope that it was his last operation on his brain but maybe he will have some plastic surgeries. He can move his legs a little bit, he has some reflexes—in bed, when you tickle his foot, he begins to take it away.

" . . . he will be a healthy boy."

And it gives me hope that everything can be OK and he will be a healthy boy.

I just wanted to share with you that before this injury, before this bullet, he was, for me . . . a genius in mechanics. Before the war he already visited inventor's school for two years . . . where they do robotics.

He likes to assemble and play with Lego and to construct cars and planes and some tanks. He draws tanks . . . *ooouuufffttt* . . . everywhere! He is one of the first ones at school who can assemble something new, who can modernize, who can add something special to his standard model . . .

I hope he can go back again next year. I think that he is a true engineer . . . of the fourth generation, because my grandfather, my father, and I are all engineers, and my brother too. . . . But unlike me he is a real engineer, I only studied as an engineer and work as a sales manager.

To compare with my younger boy, it is not his skill at all. It is better for him to run and rearrange things and talk with people. He is another boy.

I love both of them.

[A year later, I met Volodymyr and Viktor again, living with their grandparents in an apartment in Kharkiv. It was the day Stanislav went to choose a gravestone for Daria. Volodymyr was walking again and playing with a toy tank. Viktor was charging around the small room, over-excited by having guests. I was inspired by their kindness, but shocked that a year had gone by and that, of course, very little had changed. Maybe it got easier each day, maybe it didn't . . .]

" . . . it gives me hope that everything can be OK . . ."

LIZA, 26

Captain, twin sister

KYIV

THROUGH A BLACKED-OUT DOOR IN ARSENALNA, an area in Kyiv that takes its name from a 1940s munitions factory, I followed Liza upstairs and down a long, Soviet-style corridor with a low ceiling, no lighting, and blacked-out windows.

Downstairs was a trendy market, with stalls selling smoothies, Aperol Spritz, and high-end street food. Upstairs, in Liza's office, was a digital clock divided into time zones, a world map stuck to a beige wall, some simple office furniture, a camp bed, and two large computer screens. "It's funny," she said, "sometimes I hear people shouting and partying down there when I am in here, about to start the night shift. . . . It runs from 8 p.m. till 8 a.m. That's my bed there." She pointed to the camp bed at the foot of her desk.

Liza graduated from Zhytomyr Institute for Military Intelligence with a red diploma, the highest possible grade. Now, she was a military captain in the State Space Agency of Ukraine. Each night she took satellite photographs all over eastern Ukraine and, working with the United States, Argentina, and European countries, provided her Ukrainian colleagues with images of tank movements and radio locations for them to analyze in the war effort.

Liza tells her story . . .

Almost all the people here are men—mostly in their forties and fifties. I was 22 when I started doing this. Everyone is friendly but it feels strange. My friends are designers, musicians, and DJs—and here I am, doing this job!

When the war started, I stayed in Kyiv while all my co-workers left—all 100 military and 200 civilian colleagues. They all went to another office of the Space Agency in Western Ukraine, near Lviv. I was the only one who stayed. My chief said that he wanted me to go with them, but I said that I wouldn't leave.

On one hand, I understand that they didn't know what to do. Nobody knew what to tell us or what we should do. But on the other hand, I felt that we must all try to do something. And I also stayed because my twin brother, Ruslan, who is also a captain in the military, is here and I didn't want to leave him.

Everyone in my department works with computer programs and intelligence. It's not physical and no one works with guns. We can do this work but we don't have to fight. After the war started I knew my work had become more significant and important for people on the battlefield. And I know they risk their lives and it . . . [**she types furiously into a translation app**] . . . "prompts" me to work harder than ever.

"I know they risk their lives . . ."

I am from Moscow. I was born there and my mom is from the Caucasus near Chechnya. I left Russia when I was three, with my mom and my brother.

My mom left the country and she lives in Wales with her boyfriend. She has lived there eight months. Oh wait, no! I forgot that we've had the war! She has lived there for a year and a half.

[**The conversation moves on to Liza's dad. Once again she types the Ukrainian word she is looking for into her computer. I read the translation before she can say it out loud, and wish I had never asked.**]

Overdose . . . in Moscow, a long time ago when I was two years old. It was a difficult situation with my dad. Mom has never forbidden me to talk to his family but I don't want to be in touch with them any more. She told me she did love him, she still loves him, and she says about him that he was her very first and very last love, even now.

We have a grandma in Russia. I'm not in touch with them though. I tried to contact them, but they . . . believe the propaganda in Russia? You know how people are. You just can't explain to them that they are not being told the truth. You must read Orwell's book *1984*—it is exactly like that. My grandma genuinely thinks that in Ukraine people are behaving in terrible ways. She thinks Ukrainian people eat babies! It's OK though as I am not close to them any more. My brother is close to them, but I am not.

[I ask if she is married. She smiles and puts her hand to her mouth, as if to whisper something. Then she laughs.]

No, I am gay, but it is a very bad thing to be in the military. It's a big problem. Although it isn't illegal to be gay in Ukraine. If they knew I was gay, I wouldn't get promoted or any other opportunities in my career. They always ask me why I'm not married. Why don't I have a boyfriend?

[Initially Liza and I agree that we will change her name for inclusion in the book, but then she proudly says, "No, no! Stick with my name and include my orientation." This shows something of her indomitable character. Ultimately she doesn't see her future in the army, and on the way back downstairs she offers me the details of a good place to go out at night, even during the war.]

"I was the only one who stayed."

SERHII, 21

Medical student

KHARKIV

UNDERGROUND, IN THE METRO STATIONS OF KHARKIV, I saw scenes that I thought were consigned to history books about World War II. To find once again in Europe, nearly a century later, that there were thousands of civilians sleeping in metro stations to avoid the Russian bombardment was deeply unsettling.

This is exactly what I saw when I visited the metro station Serpnia 23 in Kharkiv. The condition of my entry was that I would take no photographs. The metro station is 50 feet underground and when I entered through the heavy, Soviet-built swing-doors, guarded by several territorial defense soldiers, the temperature dropped dramatically. There was a stale smell all around. From the soldiers I learnt that during the day the station was relatively empty, its residents venturing outside to check the world is still there, to see if their homes are still standing. In the evening, though, the platform filled up with at least 400 people; mainly a mixture of children and women, many of them elderly with numerous pets. I watched them all take their places in this unsuitable dormitory.

On either side of the platform were two stationary blue and yellow trains. Inside these carriages, all along the platform as well as up the steps, the floor was covered in a patchwork quilt of bright colors. Mattresses, bedding, and blankets from Ukrainian homes covered every surface; roll mats, pet boxes, and cushions sat on wooden pallets to keep people off the cold stone floor.

Serhii, a 21-year-old medical student, had set up a makeshift walk-in clinic in a room that used to be used for the station's trash. His encampment consisted of a stool, a stethoscope, and old fruit boxes full of medicine. "One for 'chest,' one for 'head,' the banana box for 'children.' The one that says 'the true delight' is the antibiotics." He laughed, but wasn't joking. Serhii had taken it upon himself to stay and treat the people in this station. It was a brave decision when you considered what might happen to him, as a young man, if he was caught by the Russians.

Interviewed March 31, 2022

Serhii tells his story . . .

I am Serhii. I am 21 years old.

Yes, I am the doctor for everything now. I am a student of Kharkiv National Medical University.

I have been living in the metro since the first day of war. February 24.

My family is in another city in the south near Mykolayiv, but right now I don't want to leave Kharkiv. Because I have never left all my life since I was five, and it is my city and I don't want to go. I know that it is my duty to be here and do my work.

It's very important because every day I have urgent patients, like those with anaphylactic shock, or a heart crisis like when the heart beats too fast. And people with burns are the hardest things I have to do. And a lot of children in the station with acute bronchitis and pneumonia.

> *"I know that it is my duty to be here and do my work."*

Yes, there are a lot of illnesses down here because it is so cold. We even have one person in the station who is one month old. They were born on February 25 in the hospital and then they came down here. She is called Diana.

We need a lot of free hands because I don't have time. I have one assistant but I need three or four because there are too many people. Because there are only two doctors here that can help. I dreamed of being a doctor when I was a little boy, I don't need a motivation because I like this work and I can do it.

Before this room was used for trash . . . it was the garbage dump. To be honest, all my life I have prepared for this moment. The boxes are for cold and flu, one for stomach, another box for heart. It was a box of apples . . . we ate them! The "true delight" box is full of antibiotics. We have a lot for children because we have lots of children. This is my food box. And this is insulin, the most expensive. There are five people, maybe six, with diabetes. We have a lot of masks for Covid but we don't have tests. I see Covid every day—but we have more important problems.

☐ **Platform living—lining up for borscht,** *Serpnia 23 Metro, Kharkiv, March 31, 2022*

☐ **Platform living,** *Serpnia 23 Metro, Kharkiv, March 31, 2022*

ANTON, 25

Helicopter pilot
POLTAVA

I MET ANTON IN POLTAVA. My meeting is specially arranged by Vitali, who works as liaison with journalists covering the war in Ukraine. Anton is a Mi-17 and Mi-24 helicopter pilot based in Poltava. He is a Captain with the 18th Separate Army Aviation Brigade. He told me "I wanted an ordinary life—to build a house, plant a tree, and raise a son". It takes so long to train a pilot to Anton's standard and each one is so valuable to the Ukrainian war effort, that I wasn't allowed to ask him any questions beyond his name and age—for fear of jeopardizing his safety. Vitali the press officer said "The value of a combat pilot is so great. Even at the end of the military pilot school a pilot wouldn't be experienced enough to fly combat missions". However, since the start of the fullscale invasion Anton has flown more than 100 missions over Bakhmut supporting the infantry fighting below to hold back the Russian advance. "I'm sorry I can't say anything interesting now, my work is equally scary, equally difficult. This has become routine. Of course, the victory of Ukraine, the end of these cruel events and a hope for a calm and happy life".

☐ **Fixing an Mi-17 helicopter of 18th Separate Army Aviation Brigade,** *Poltava, March 20, 2023*

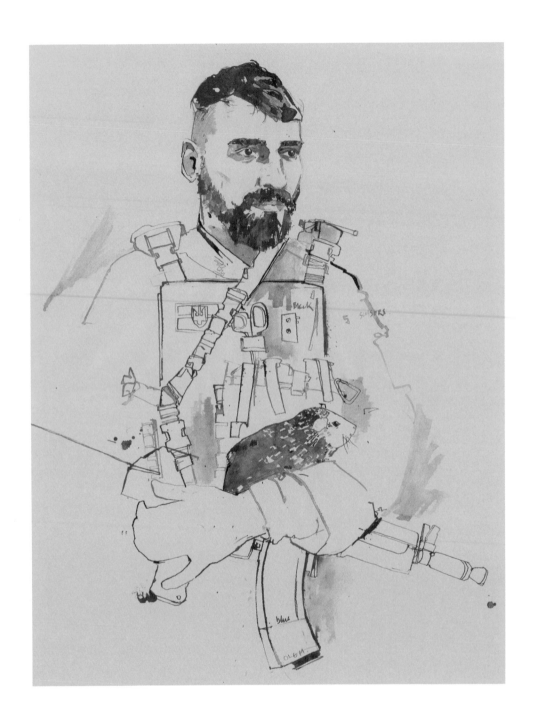

OLEG, 26

Soccer fan, volunteer medic

KHARKIV

OLEG IS A 26-YEAR-OLD "ULTRA" SOCCER FAN, an artist, and a book collector. His dream, he told me, was to own a restaurant combined with a bookshop. And he showed me some of his favorite designs.

His Ukrainian Army uniform and the "ultra" fan image were at odds with the drawing I was making of Oleg—which showed him holding his pet guinea pig, Almond, given to him by his girlfriend and now perching on his AK-47. "You are a big pig," he said affectionately.

Oleg tells his story . . .

On February 24, at 5 a.m., I woke up to the sound of explosions. For a few seconds I thought it was thunder, but then I realized that the war had started after all. These were missile strikes on military facilities located outside the city. My apartment is near the outskirts in the Saltivka district, which was experiencing the greatest destruction in the city. Then I packed up and left for my parents' and together with them we left for a safer place in the city center, which would be their home for the next few months.

I cannot say that I predicted the beginning of the war. But everything around pointed to exactly that. A few days before the start, I lived in conflict, because I didn't understand what was the point of continuing with my usual life if everything was going to start soon. And on the morning of the 24th, everything fell into place. In an instant, most of the things that worried me before and were important lost their meaning altogether.

For the first seconds, of course, I felt fear, because the first sounds of explosions were very loud and it was not clear what exactly was being fired upon. Then I felt a certain drive due to the influx of adrenaline, because there was no time to think, it was necessary to act quickly. And when I was in a safe place with my family, I felt a certain relief. But in general, everyone felt tremendous tension, because people were destroying their usual way of life.

I did not question whether to leave Ukraine or not. I clearly knew that I would fight for my country and city. As for my parents, I asked them to leave before and after, but they didn't want to. And I respect and accept their choice, because they also joined the struggle and helped as much as they could, worked with journalists, helped people, etc.

The Simmer Polecats Crew [SPC] is an association or "firm," as they say in England, of ultras of Kharkiv Metalist Football Club, which has existed since 2009. We actively supported our team, went

" . . . most of the things that worried me before and were important lost their meaning altogether."

to away matches, did performances, painted graffiti, participated in fights. Since 2014, ultras of Ukraine have shown themselves to be one of the strongest pro-Ukrainian subcultures. Many fans have become the backbone of the most combat-ready units. Our team was no exception: many of our guys took part in military operations from the age of fourteen. Even in 2022, our team unites us despite the fact that we are fighting in different divisions. We are working in many directions to covertly provide for our boys and contribute our share to the victory of Ukraine.

Originally we wanted our name to be "Sinner" but the man making the badges got the translation wrong, so we had no choice. We adopted the idea of "simmering" with pride.

I have been in the team since I was thirteen and for me it is a second family. We have known each other for many years; we have had many adventures and challenges together. In war, it is very important to have people you know and trust. We often feel that our own soccer path has been preparing us for war.

In 2017, I underwent basic training with a group called the Hospitallers, a volunteer organization of paramedics. It was founded by Yana Zinkevych at the beginning of the hostilities in Ukraine in 2014. We help the armed forces to evacuate the wounded at all stages. Some of the boys from the SPC joined the ranks of the Hospitallers and participated in the Kyiv company. Later they joined us in Kharkiv and I started working with them. I formally joined the ranks in the summer of 2022. I learned from my colleagues and took various courses and practices. I am not a medic and it should be understood that they should not work in the first stages of evacuation, because their knowledge makes them very valuable personnel who can save many lives in the hospital. Therefore, such positions are often filled by fighters who have undergone basic pre-medical training. We rely on advanced American protocols and try to constantly improve our own learning. Now absolutely everyone

". . . our own football path has been preparing us for war."

☐ **Selling second-hand things at Rynok Starykh Rechey Market,** *Kharkiv, March 12, 2023*

in our country has to go through first-aid training; it doesn't matter if you are a soldier or a civilian.

A normal day at war is usually a tense wait at the position that you will be called for evacuation. You can sit for many days without work, and in one day have several dozen wounded. This is difficult, but very important work. I admire and am very proud of my colleagues, who save dozens of lives every day across the front.

We worked with the 92nd Brigade from the outskirts of Kharkiv and farther to the Kharkiv region towards the border. These locations were Mala Rohan, Vilkhivka, Sorokivka, Shestakovo, Peremoha.

One day we had a long and difficult evacuation from a very hot place. We were carrying several wounded, one of whom had a partial leg amputation. I held on to the body with one hand and on to his leg with the other. All the way I told him that we had almost arrived, but he knew and told me that I was brazenly lying to him and that he didn't like that very much! But we successfully transported him and transferred him to a medevac with our Hospitallers from Sweden.

The most inspiring period was the Kharkiv counteroffensive. I saw the liberated territories of our region, the cities we had visited, the villages where I spent my childhood. It was very important for us to prove to everyone and the enemy that they will not stay here.

"This is difficult, but very important work."

☐ **Night raids with Kharkiv Police,** *Kharkiv, April 3, 2022*

NATA, 34 & ARTEM, 14

Screenwriter & son

MARIUPOL

ON MARCH 4, 2022, as the fighting intensified in Mariupol, Nata moved her family into her mother's basement. There were five of them: Nata, her son Artem [left], her husband, her mom, and her mother-in-law. Only four of them would leave, 25 days later.

For several weeks in 2022, Mariupol, a previously little-known town of over 400,000 people, monopolised news headlines around the world. The news told us of the atrocities being carried out there, but it was difficult to imagine the extent of the horror. Russian misinformation clouded the story and it was impossible to get an accurate picture of the situation in a town besieged by Russian forces.

But for Nata and Artem this story was theirs as they had lived it, without sensation or exaggeration. They would have shared it with anyone that day. I just happened to be sitting in front of them in a café in Kyiv.

Nata tells their story . . .

At the beginning of March 2022, Mariupol's lights, communications, internet, water, heating, and gas were cut off. The countdown began for the city and its residents. My husband, my son, my mother, and mother-in-law and I had already moved to my mother's apartment, since it was dangerous to hide in our house. At first, the Russians shelled non-residential buildings: schools, stores, pharmacies, and shopping centers. Our house was vibrating, with plaster falling off the walls. We took blankets, chairs, backpacks of essential items and went down to the basement. We thought we needed to stay there for one night, but it turned out we were there for a month.

"All of them were in a state of shock."

The basement was dark and cold. Narrow passageways led in different directions off a small corridor. On each side were compartments like in a train, only instead of partitions each was divided by uneven blocks of concrete. The ceiling was five feet high in some places and the floor was piled high with dust, garbage, and old pipes. We occupied two compartments and built a shared recliner for my mother-in-law and the baby. I made myself a seat out of cardboard boxes. My husband lay on the floor.

The next day the shelling intensified. We went and got food and other necessities and brought them to the basement. Two stools became our dining table. A cardboard box became a grocery cabinet. In all, there were about 30 people in the basement as well as us, including several small children. Around us, the city was erupting into hell and chaos. Every time I went to the entrance of the shelter, I saw more and more columns of black smoke. Our military allowed us to take food and water from the bombed-out stores. Risking their lives, people ventured out and began to stock up on provisions, but not everyone returned from such missions. Looters also appeared and, like locusts, they swarmed into bombed-out malls, supermarkets, restaurants, and offices. They took everything they could: tires, car parts, building materials, televisions, refrigerators, clothes, and gold.

During that first week and between periods of shelling, if possible we left the basement to find food. Our diet at that time included baked potatoes, pasta, leftover meat, and canned food. We ate in small portions, twice a day. But there were five of us and we soon ran out of food. From time to time my husband went to the bombed-out stores to see if he could replenish supplies, but the shops were often empty. Water was the hardest thing to come by.

This terrible situation lasted for more than a week. One day, in front of our eyes, we saw planes approaching us. The first plane flew over the yard and dropped its missiles. The explosion blew my husband into an entrance hall and by a miracle he wasn't killed by a jagged metal door. In this explosion, a neighbor died at the other end of the house when his leg was blown off. The second missile hit was closer and blew the front of the apartments out. I can still hear the rumble, the sound of shattering glass, and the screams of terror in my ears. People who had stayed in their apartments began to rush to the basement. All of them were in a state of shock. Some were naked, others held babies in their arms, shaking with horror and looking for shelter. People kept repeating the phrase, "That's it! The apartment is gone! There's nothing!"

"It felt like an eternity."

The door of our neighbors on the fifth floor jammed. They called for help, but no one heard them. When it calmed down a little, people helped out. All the time, the shelling continued. An airstrike hit the house across the street and people were killed when a fire broke out and the door to the shelter was jammed. Dozens of people were trapped. One man ran to help and was hit by shrapnel in his back. Others came and managed to free the inhabitants. A nurse was among them and she stitched up the wounds with no anaesthetic. It was a night of hell! We sat for hours in the basement in pitch blackness, terrified by every new explosion. It felt like an eternity.

One by one, the houses around us burned and collapsed. Leaving the basement was tantamount to suicide! It was impossible even to go to the end of the house to pick up the body of a neighbor who had been killed early on in the conflict. Five people died in the house. They were all elderly and unable physically to get down to the shelter. One day, when we looked out from our basement, we saw our apartment from afar. It was on fire. I realized that we no longer had our own place! I did not want to cry, I did not want to waste my energy on emotions. At that time the only thing I wanted was to survive! All resources of my body were used for that! All material things became unimportant!

The most frightening thing was the rumble of the planes. We knew when we heard an airplane flying, there would be three or four missile drops. We prayed the bombs wouldn't hit our house. We sighed with relief every time one missed. But at the same time, we knew that "missed" was just hitting another house somewhere else. And there were people there, too, just like us.

At the time, the temperature was below freezing, with wind, snow, and rain. We dressed in everything we had with us, wrapped ourselves in blankets, but we were still cold. Our only salvation was hot tea. We had to light a fire with wood for several hours under heavy firefights to get the water to boil. We hardly ate anything. In the morning I made tea for everybody and steamed some oatmeal. In the afternoon we shared some cookies and for supper we had sardines. We divided one can between five of us to save money. We rarely left the cellar. We didn't eat much, we didn't socialize much, and we became irritable, nervous. We didn't even have the strength to support one another morally. We survived on animal fear and instinct. We were running out of candles and began to make candlesticks. It was especially difficult for my mother-in-law, at 84, to live in such conditions.

"I did not want to cry, I did not want to waste my energy on emotions."

I wanted to yell, "Stop it! Stop this hell! We don't have any more strength!"

When our neighborhood was overrun by the Russians, the shelling shifted to a neighboring square. The danger did not go away, we could still be hit in the yard, but it happened less often. Dirty and exhausted, we gradually began to leave the basement for trips outside. We stayed close to the door and ran inside at the first sound of any bombardment or the rumble of an airplane. The first thing we did was to collect the bodies of the dead and take them behind the garages. The ground was absolutely frozen. One by one, we buried them in the yard behind the house.

We were short of firewood—one of the basic necessities of life—so we started saving it. We collected it where we could find it and took it into apartments, storing it between floors to keep it from getting too cold. The second vital necessity was water. We looked for it everywhere. We took it from drains, collected rainwater, and thawed the snow.

We were hungry. We still had some food, but we had to economize, because we didn't know when we would be able to replenish our supplies. One day, I remember I found some frozen potatoes on the balcony. Potatoes were a luxury at the time. Everyone had long since run out of vegetables. While my husband went to find water, I decided to bake some. The shelling started nearby. I thought, "They shouldn't be shooting at us any more." Everyone ran into the basement, but I stood on the doorstep, thinking, "Don't hit the grill! I so want potatoes!" Then I couldn't bear it any more and ran to get them.

The DNR [Donetsk People's Republic] military began to walk around the neighborhood in groups. Passing through our yard for the first time, they were surprised to see so many people still left in the city. They lowered their eyes when we said, "Men, what have you done!" They replied, "Man, we tried to be careful, but it didn't work." Gradually, their attitude changed. They started acting rudely, blaming us for everything.

[Before the interview, Nata had provided her testimony in full via WhatsApp. At this point I ask if she would prefer for me read it so she doesn't have to relive the trauma. How wrong I was. She looks upset and tells me she must read it herself, and that she wants many people to know the story of Mariupol. It is clear that there is great personal value for Nata in sharing this story out loud. She is briefly unburdened by knowing that others will also know what happened.]

And then disaster struck. My mother-in-law didn't feel well. Her body could not withstand living in these inhumane conditions. We fought to keep her alive as best we could. There was no medical help in the city and the hospitals only took the

"Potatoes were a luxury at the time."

wounded. I remember my mother-in-law craving bread, but we hadn't had bread for two months. My husband went to see if he could find some humanitarian aid. He was gone for a whole day. When he came back towards evening, he was covered in blood with a bandage on his head. He had been hit by something near the hospital. They had stitched him up without any anaesthetic. The next day we managed to buy medicine and get some humanitarian aid. There was a loaf of bread in it. "Mom, I brought you bread!" my husband said. But it was too late, my mother-in-law was dying. For hours my husband sat by her side, holding her hand.

We called the neighbors and they helped bury her. We had no ceremonies, funerals, or other proper rituals. They buried her in the front yard, under the window.

"There was pain and doom in their eyes."

In the first days of April, we decided to leave the basement and spend the night at my mother's apartment. The door was always open so it wouldn't jam. The windows were open so they wouldn't blow out. It was freezing cold. I wore a hat, two warm sweatsuits, a turtleneck, a sweater, and a jacket. I didn't take those clothes off for a month. All that time, I only brushed my teeth a couple of times to save water. My hands were black with soot. There was no water to wash.

One day, shivering with cold, I took off my hat to comb my hair and strands of hair were left on the comb. I tried not to look in the mirror.

Once, when it rained heavily, we collected a lot of water. We allowed ourselves a few pints every day for the four of us to wash. We saved the water and used it to flush the toilet later. Closer to the middle of April, I couldn't stand being so dirty any longer and decided to take a bath. I washed in a bowl in the kitchen. It was freezing and the water was black.

Every day was the same. I got up at 6 a.m., fired up the grill, boiled water, got something to eat, refilled the firewood stock, and set off in search of food. The parking lot in front of the Metro [the former shopping center] was where trucks with food, humanitarian supplies, field kitchens, medicine, and water first arrived.

The first time we went it was not easy. We had to navigate burned and destroyed homes, charred cars and buses, torn wires, craters, and debris. We saw crosses in front yards. But the worst thing of all was seeing the rubble everywhere and knowing there must be dead people lying underneath. I wanted to be sick.

When we got to the Metro it was just as terrible. Outside the gates stood several thousand people, all looking shrivelled and pale, with overgrown hair and dressed in baggy clothes. There was pain and doom in their eyes. People stood in lines: one for humanitarian aid, one for paid food, one for medicine. Each person had a number on their hand. We found a line for food and signed in. We were number 642. When they opened the gates, there was a stampede to the trucks. Some people fell down. The military started shooting in the air, but people still ran. Later that evening, when I had stood in line for five hours without getting anything, I understood why they were running.

The food situation in the city at that time was VERY difficult. Once a month we were given a small loaf of bread, a gallon of water, four cans of meat, four cans of food, two cans of condensed milk, a couple of packs of pasta and porridge, sugar, flour, and sunflower oil each by the authorities. This might sound normal, but try eating just this for a month. The bread lasted for a couple of days, the stew was horrible, the sardines were even worse. The pasta was boiled and the condensed milk was inedible.

Of course, it was enough to stop us from starving to death, but after a month in the basement, I was desperate for real food. The only place we could get it was the trucks and we had to pay for it. They had bread, sausage, milk, cookies, and butter. But there wasn't enough for everyone. The vendors didn't ration the amount of goods per person, so it was first come, first served. Finally, on the third day, we ran too and we got a sausage stick! The prices were inflated and they only accepted cash. The sellers looked down on us and were rude. They yelled, "If you complain, you'll go to the back of the line. So we stood silently in line, hoping for sausages and bread all day long.

". . . it was enough to stop us from starving to death . . ."

One day at the Metro, they were handing out Phoenix phone starter packs. The line was several thousand people long. We were searched by soldiers with machine guns. The only way of charging the phone was by standing in another mile-long line. On April 17, I managed to get on the internet. It was only possible at the Metro and it took me 20 attempts. One by one, messages arrived.

People had remembered me. They were looking for me. That was the moment that I realized I had survived. We decided to leave. Once the decision was made, it was only a matter of time, but it was not that simple.

We were in Russian territory, and it was only possible to enter the territory controlled by Ukraine by personal transport, through fifteen Russian checkpoints. We did not have a car at that time because it had been destroyed during the shelling. So we hoped for a miracle. Then the information about the evacuation came. At the appointed time we arrived at the assembly area. There were already about 200 people waiting for buses. Among them were children, old people, and the disabled. Instead of the bus, we got an APC [armored personnel carrier]. The soldiers got out of the APC and turned on a video camera. They started chanting, "WARNING! WARNING! Threat of missile attack! TAKE COVER!" and continued without stopping. Some people moved a few yards away but most stayed despite their fear.

"People had remembered me. They were looking for me."

While all this was going on, soldiers were quietly smoking at the nearest checkpoint. Thousands of other people were waiting at the Metro. And we were the only ones getting harassed! For wanting to enter Ukrainian territory! When the soldiers left, everyone went back to the bus stop and waited there until evening. Deep in our hearts we knew that there would be no buses that day.

We had our next chance on April 25. Acquaintances showed us a place where a driver waits and offers to drive to Berdyansk for a fee. "The price is 8000 hryvnias [UAH]," he said. "In two hours you will be in Berdyansk! Let's go!" We were not spontaneous usually, but this time we decided to do it, because there were rumors that the city would be closed. The driver took detours around most of the checkpoints, along unpaved roads, through an abandoned cemetery, passing abandoned cars. At last we were let go and an hour later we pulled into Berdyansk. It was like another world. The driver took us to a hotel, assuring us that there were buses to Zaporizhzhia from the city almost daily. We decided to spend the night in normal conditions and move on the next day.

All our previous daily routine now seemed unbelievable as we experienced snow-white sheets, an electric kettle, fresh water in the tap, clean towels. A hot shower was the height of bliss. For the first time in months I was warm and clean. The next day we found out that buses to Zaporizhzhia didn't run for two weeks, so we stayed in Berdyansk for almost a month.

Life in the occupied city was not easy. Prices were outrageous and shops were empty. Cards were only accepted in a few stores and getting cash cost 15%. A couple of weeks later, there was a rumor that a Red Cross evacuation motorcade was coming from Azovstal. It was supposed to go through the Lunacharsky Ring [a place not far from Berdyansk], to pick up people who wanted to leave on the way. This was our first opportunity to leave. More than 500 people gathered on the track outside the city and waited all day. We were told that the motorcade was on its way from Azovstal and would be with us soon. We waited, anticipating that in a few hours we would be in Zaporizhzhia. But, alas, the motorcade passed without stopping. There were ten buses! Three of them were empty and the rest were only one-third full. Disheartened, we went back to Berdyansk.

Our second attempt was to join a cortege of six buses with Red Cross signs. The price list was 2000 UAH per person. There were fifteen checkpoints. At each checkpoint the men were taken out for inspection. We stopped on the highway before Vasylivka with three more Russian checkpoints to go. We were 30 miles from Zaporizhzhia. We were number 67 in the line. During the day the line grew to 300. Not a single car or bus was allowed through.

"Life in the occupied city was not easy."

"My body was breaking— we were walking like zombies."

We stayed overnight on the highway. There were more than a thousand of us. We only had the water and food that we took with us. The lavatory was in a shelter under a bush. We heard shooting from time to time in the far distance. It was worse at night. We woke up to a terrible roar of guns. The sky was shining like a thunderstorm. Panic broke out, people ran out of the buses and cars, hiding in the ravines. We sat in terror, knowing there might be retaliation. On the second day, another 500 cars joined the line. A woman died on one of the buses. Her heart failed. We spent a second night on the highway. That day it rained, which made the situation much more difficult.

A day later we made our third attempt to leave. On social media I saw an ad for a private passenger car for 24,000 US dollars for four people. The following morning we drove to Vasylivka. During the day about 200 cars gathered again, as well as fifteen vans with vegetables. To keep us out of sight, all the cars were moved a distance from the checkpoint, to a battered gas station along the road. Once again, no one was allowed to pass the checkpoints. We spent another night on the highway. The three of us slept in the backseat of the car. Or rather I didn't sleep—I just held the cat, so as not to disturb the driver. Every half an hour she would ask to go outside. In order not to dirty the car, I took her out and she started hunting.

The following morning, there was talk that no one would get through in the next five days. Our driver began to try other options, such as taking a detour through the fields. But we decided the risk was too great, everything was mined. Just a couple of days before, a car on such a road blew up on a mine. We decided to wait and spent a second sleepless night on the highway. By morning, we were desperate for proper food. The locals brought sausage for 150 UAH per pound, bread for 30 UAH, cigarettes of poor quality for 100 UAH, a gallon of water 60 UAH, and Snickers for 100 UAH. We spent our third sleepless night on the track. The driver went crazy. We managed to persuade him to spend another night. It was the fourth night on the route. My body was breaking—we were walking like zombies. The driver said, "That's it, I didn't sign up for this, I'm going home after a few more hours! Are you coming with me?" Even though the prospect of the four of us staying on the highway with our suitcases and cat was really bad, we refused to leave anyway. We were saved by a stroke of luck. After the driver left, we walked around the parking lot and found a half-empty minibus that had four spare seats.

Half an hour later we saw some movement in the parking lot. Some Dagestanis arrived from a block post and brought tea and porridge with stewed meat. Everyone was so hungry that they ate their food in five minutes. They couldn't get enough. Then the military tried to persuade us not to go to Ukraine. They advised us to go to Russia. In the end, they promised that at 5 p.m. they would allow ten cars through. They didn't lie! At exactly 5 p.m. the first ten cars entered Vasylivka. At 7.30 p.m. we moved. We passed into Vasylivka across two checkpoints. At the third we were told to go back 500 yards and to wait for another day. So we spent the night in the grey zone. This was our fifth night on the road. We were a group of ten cars in a war zone. There was a fresh shell crater on the road next to us and we were surrounded by several burnt-out vehicles. We were so exhausted that we didn't even have the strength to be afraid.

The next day dragged on endlessly. Finally, at 5 p.m. they started letting us through. A few miles later and we were finally in territory under Ukrainian control!

"We were so exhausted that we didn't even have the strength to be afraid."

ANDRII & OLEKSANDR
40th Artillery Brigade
NEAR KUPYANSK

THE RUSSIAN POSITIONS WERE 5 MILES AWAY. A muddy path cut through the unharvested sunflowers, across the damp, beige landscape and into a tall hedge about 400 yards ahead of us. From a distance, it wasn't clear what we were heading towards. As we got closer, however, there were signs of life—the detritus from weeks of living on the edge was all around. Then I heard the voices of members of the 40th Artillery Brigade below us and saw a filthy staircase that led underground, into a six foot deep bunker ahead. Once we were inside, I saw the roof was made up of tree trunks covered in thick soil, so as to remain camouflaged from enemy drones.

Empty fuel canisters, broken wooden pallets, and used shell casings lay on the floor. I could see that there was no time here for anything other than fighting—no time for doing anything more than what was absolutely necessary. By the looks of things, any distractions would have been fatal.

Andrii, Oleksandr, Kostyantyn, and Vitalii welcomed us into their bunker (another soldier slept through our entire visit). The space was lit by a single electric bulb, and the roof was just low enough for no one to be able to stand up properly. Silver matting, the sort you might put on your car windscreen in winter, was nailed into the mud walls. There was a small bench for cooking and around the edge was a mud platform, where they all slept. Cooking pots lay dirty on the floor, alongside baby wipes half out of their packets. Next to the Kalashnikovs there stood a small pile of wood, waiting to be burned.

However, it was the smell in the bunker that indicated more strongly than perhaps anything I have ever experienced that the normal rules and priorities of life counted for nothing. This was another dimension. This was a place where the only measure of a day was to be alive at the end of it, and to fall asleep before you had time to think about it. To get away from it all.

As I looked around the bunker, full of cigarette smoke, I could feel the adrenaline. That was the real drug of choice that morning, evident in the wide, searching and tormented eyes of one man in particular—Andrii. He started to talk to me.

Interviewed March 15, 2023

Andrii tells his story . . .

This morning there was a hit, so we are all a bit stressed now. We were here underground, but it hit so hard that we were thrown to the walls.

I hate the Russians. They killed my cousin Dima—he was serving in Azov. He was young and cool. I'm an orphan. All I have is my brother, sister, and cousins. I also have a wife and an eight-month-old son in Mykolaiv Oblast, but I'm here. The Russians are killing us. I could die at any time. I went home for six days in December—that's all.

I was studying in Odesa, reading Technology. As soon as the war started in 2014, I joined the army. I was in Popasna, Pisky, serving in Kulchytsky Battalion, I was an ATO [Ammunition technical officer] for six years and then I came here to Kupyansk. I'm a veteran of the war at 28 years old.

I'll be honest with you: the war won't finish in 2023. You know why? Even if we manage to counterattack and push them back, we'll have to stay on the border for several years. And even if Putin dies, a new one will replace him.

> *". . . even if Putin dies, a new one will replace him."*

[As Andrii is speaking a discussion is going on in this dark foxhole. It sounds serious. How long could they spend here now that the Russians know their position and would shell again soon? Could they risk being out in the open and dragging their M777 artillery piece to a new location, or should they wait underground and hope the Russians kept missing? Making the wrong decision with these sorts of impossible questions could get you killed in an instant. And anyone who thought otherwise was either mad or already dead.

Next to Andrii, an enormous man called Oleksandr watches quietly and smiles at me reassuringly.]

Oleksandr tells his story . . .

Before the war I was transferring cars from America to Europe. Then I felt I couldn't be abroad. I have to be here. We're here by contract. I volunteered to work with animals.

We evacuated the Feldman [Ecopark] zoo in [the outskirts of] Kharkiv in 2022—it was one or two miles from the Russian positions. It was very difficult. It was like this: we were in civilian clothes, red-and-yellow jackets, so we were easy to see. First, we sedated the wolf so he was asleep, and carried him on our backs. Then suddenly we saw a drone nearby and I said, "F***, it will get hot now," and they started to shoot. They could see we were civilians, but they kept shooting anyway. We dodged the bullets and got the animals out. We took them to Kharkiv and then to Dnipro. We've been working as animal volunteers for seven years, so we knew where to go with them. Each time we passed a checkpoint, our soldiers there were shocked. We opened the car for inspection and there was a wolf on the backseat!

One of the most painful moments was when the Russians were shooting us and a shot went directly into the monkeys' cage. The poor creatures cried so loudly, it was very painful to hear. The most terrifying thing was that they sounded like people.

" . . . there was a wolf on the backseat!"

My family knew that I'd join the army one day. I told them that first I'd volunteer to work with animals and then I'd go into the army.

The main difference between us and the Russians is that we care about people's lives.

You know, I've got quite used to this life. Adrenaline is a very powerful stimulant. I spoke to a friend of mine who is also in combat and he said, "We'll miss this in the future." He's right. When I first came here, I shuddered every time the artillery gun was fired, and now I'm used to it. We shoot at Lancet drones. Yesterday the guys destroyed four Uragan rocket launchers.

This morning was tough, because they hit us. Two hours afterwards, we got the coordinates where we should aim to hit them back. So, if they start firing again we will need to move very quickly. Russians have counter-battery radar called Zoopark. It's a radar that can find where we are. We're lucky if we get to stay in the same place for a week. Often we arrive and then the shooting starts and we need to move again.

I have relatives in Russia. One of my cousins moved from Luhansk to Russia and got married there. They support Ukraine in this conflict—for example,

☐ **Underground with the
40th Artillery Brigade,**
near Kupyansk, March 15, 2023

they think Crimea is Ukrainian, but they went on holiday to Abkhazia [a separatist region in Georgia aligned with Russia]. It's crazy, when the war is here! I asked them, "Are you mad?" All these years they were coming.

I have lots of friends in Kharkiv—many are volunteers, although I have others. Now when I open Facebook it's very painful. Many are very close friends and lots of them are dead now. On the other hand, sometimes war creates opportunities for new meetings! I've met so many dear people near Kupyansk and I'm sure we'll win this war.

The Russians say that the Ukrainian brigades in Bakhmut only live for a maximum of three or four days. Whether that's true or not, we have suffered huge losses there. Since February we've only had a two-week break. Human resources are limited and soldiers can't go on rotation, because we don't have enough soldiers. It's a tragedy that young guys are dying while lots of men are sitting in the cities, hiding. My brother is like this. He served in the army, but doesn't want to be mobilized. He sits at home and is frightened in case he receives a mobilization letter . . . If he had the chance he would leave Ukraine and go abroad.

[At the end of the visit Andrii grabs my head with both hands and pulls me into both shoulders in a passionate embrace. It is as if I wasn't going to be allowed to forget them. He then rips the military badges off his shoulders and thrusts them into my hands. The look in his eyes has stayed with me ever since.]

". . . we have suffered huge losses there."

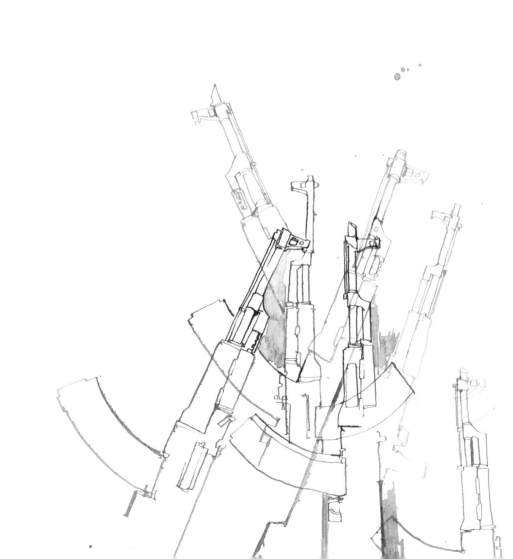

FOR 155 PROP

DO N1T
TRANSPORT

CHARGE IN A
VERTICAL

☐ M777 howitzer 155 mm camouflaged and
waiting for action, *near Kupyansk, March 15, 2023*

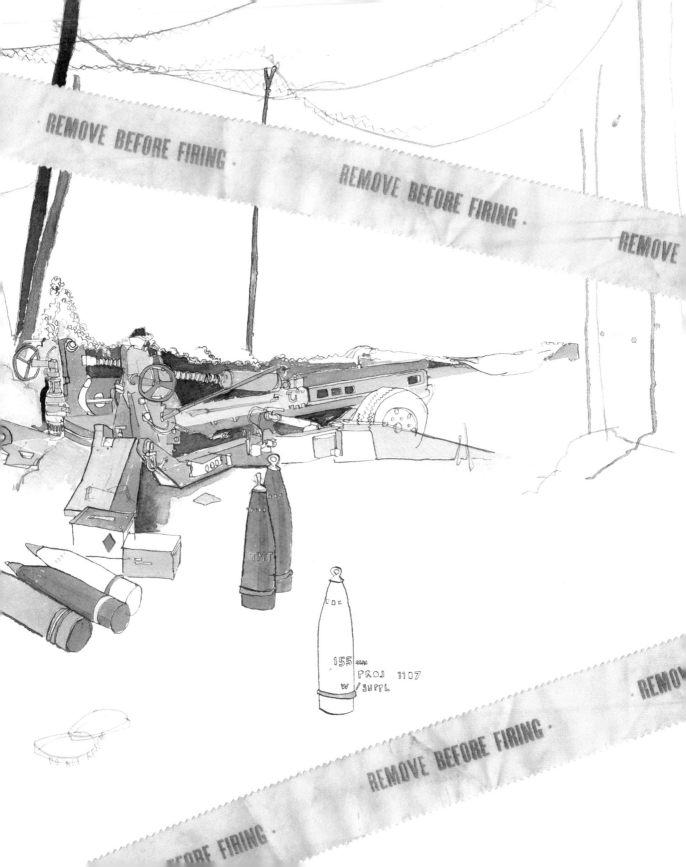

VOLODYMYR, 30

Ex-hooligan, soldier, father

DRUZHKIVKA

IN 1986, ONE OF THE REACTORS AT CHORNOBYL Nuclear Power Plant in northern Ukraine exploded, launching radioactive particles into the air in the world's worst ever nuclear accident.

At the time, in a nearby town, Iryna was living with her husband. Six years later she gave birth to Volodymyr. Now 30, he told me how his thyroid cancer was a direct result of this accident years before he was born. Having cancer had left him with a difficult choice: should he stay or should he leave?

In a small house in Druzhkivka, I drew Volodymyr lying on his bed, with his daughter Anya's toy dinosaur lying on his chest. He was wearing a "Don't Stop the Hooligans" T-shirt, from his days as a Dynamo Kyiv fan. He wasn't going to let history repeat itself: Anya, aged four, is far away from the danger, in Poland. Volodymyr was from Kostyantynivka, but he had been fighting in the trenches near Bakhmut with the Anti-Tank Unit of the 3rd Assault Brigade. In each of the rooms of the house, tired figures lay on roll mats on the floor. They used their belongings as a pillow and marked their space with their rucksacks. And like all people in war, they waited and slept. While Volodymyr waited he thought about his daughter, who he was going see in a few months.

Interviewed March 18 & August 28, 2023

Volodymyr tells his story . . .

I was born in 1992 into a family of programmers and engineers: Iryna and Oleksandr, my parents, worked at the state railway company their whole lives. They were born in Konotop, and they later witnessed the accident at the Chornobyl Nuclear Power Plant, the collapse of the USSR, and the long-awaited "birth" of independent Ukraine.

When I was five, I remember my father jumping around the room while watching a soccer game on TV. Later I discovered that that day, Dynamo Kyiv beat Barcelona 3–0. Later that year we did it again. Dynamo Kyiv was the love of my father and of the city, so deciding to support them was easy. I became a real soccer hooligan, with all its subculture. We created chaos and we challenged the political system with it. It was a great time. There are lots of us ultras and hooligans fighting together on the frontline. Now colors and ideological convictions don't divide us, because we are united around the future of Ukraine.

> "... we are united around the future of Ukraine."

After high school, I was kicked out of university because I missed a retake. I was invited to register for the military. I did not want to serve in the "old army," so I thought $200 would solve my issue and I deferred. Nevertheless, at the medical examining board I had an ultrasound and they found a malignant tumor in my thyroid gland. Then I had surgery, chemotherapy, and isolation in a medical ward behind a heavy lead door, along with books by Nietzsche, Kafka, and Castaneda. That period of my life has been literally erased from my memory, but it seems to me that I changed a lot in that time.

After February 2022, I decided to stay to fight because it was the right thing to do; any country is its people. We sing the national anthem and we celebrate Independence Day, showing honor and respect for the state. How can you live a good and peaceful life somewhere in Europe or America, knowing that you abandoned your native land? How can you be a hypocrite? The first days of the invasion were full of the heroism and courage of the Ukrainian people. At the time we thought we were about to die, but we were ready to fight. Even unarmed civilians lay down in front of the tanks and blocked the military advances of occupying troops! It was incredible. I could never have watched on from the wings. I would stop respecting myself forever.

The day before the 24th we shared the news and discussed the situation, and at night, I could not sleep. You know how on New Year's Eve, you feel the holiday "in the air". So it was on the eve of the invasion, the air sparked with anxiety.

When I was about to go to bed, I heard the first explosions from afar. I did not believe it was happening immediately. I grabbed the necessary things and documents, filled the car and went to the house of my ex-wife and daughter. I tried for several hours to persuade them to leave and go to Poland. At that time, in their house, you would have been forgiven for thinking it was an ordinary day. . . . But the newsreader's voice and the rocket explosions soon reminded us that nothing was normal that morning.

I already knew then that I would join a group of my friends, veterans of the Azov regiment. I knew I would go to war, to another world I knew nothing about. I knew I was saying goodbye to my home and my world—goodbye to my daughter. It was always hard for me to say goodbye after the weekends we spent together, and I often cried sitting in the car when she closed the door of her mother's house. Now I recall that moment with great bitterness. Then I returned to Kyiv and signed up. For a long time the school became our barracks, until the Russian army was pushed back from Kyiv.

"... on the eve of the invasion, the air sparked with anxiety."

In general the days at war were chaos, permeated with army order, courage, and fear. Once I was sent from the trenches, alone in the middle of the night, to meet a reinforcement group. I'm a bespectacled man who tries not to drive at night, I did not know the road, and even if I had known it, I still wouldn't have been able to see anything. It was an unusually dark night, and neither the stars nor the moon were out. Nothing was visible at all—there was only a field, an open area, disturbed by armored vehicle tracks and covered with pits from shells. I literally groped my way to the place. I was trying to forget about snipers and avoid the flags marking the mines. I didn't have my radio with me and I thought that our troops would shoot me—and they should have! I tried to shout quietly to those I was looking for. I cursed and cursed everyone in the world and myself for agreeing on this stupid idea. In the end, I lived to tell the tale. But war is unpredictable, full of surprises, and often depends on the actions of your enemy and your luck. And, for some, it becomes their last days.

My daughter is the most precious and valuable thing I have, but someone has to do this job. Doctors treat people, firefighters put out fires, teachers teach, and soldiers fight. Now I am an experienced military man. I despise and hate war to the core, but it is not over yet. It's impossible to give up halfway, or our friends will have died for nothing and their children would have cried for nothing.

"I despise and hate war to the core, but it is not over yet."

Our unit is called the 3rd Separate Assault Brigade, based on our former unit of the "Azov Kyiv" special operations forces. We are infantry working in Bakhmut.

God, it was cold in Bakhmut. We entered the positions in winter. The trenches had to be dug with a pickaxe because the ground was like rock. It was permafrost. The area was open with a strong wind and it was freezing at night; some guys left with frostbite. It was impossible to warm up. After each shift, we hid in a dugout and snuggled up to a friend. Waking up after a couple of hours of awful sleep, we found that our weapons were frozen, and if you were inattentive and did not keep the water close then it would be frozen. Trench candles and chemical heating pads saved us—but even my moustache was covered with ice!

I saw my daughter Anya this year and she did not immediately recognise me! Then, of course, we had a wonderful time together. Now she and my ex-wife live in Poland and, it seems, are not going to come back. It is very unpleasant for me to think about it, but as long as we have a war going on, I cannot stop them from going abroad to be safe.

I have no messages for the Russians. It's a futile exercise. Nevertheless, I sincerely believe that we will win, and then we will definitely never forget the help of our friends, who did not let the tyrant destroy our country and our people. And if this happens, please all visit us in a beautiful, peaceful, free Ukraine. It's good out here. It was and will definitely be again.

"It's good out here.
It was and will definitely be again."

☐ **Wartime customers at the supermarket,** *Druzhkivka, March 18, 2023*

ANDRII

Volunteer

KUPYANSK

THE MOST DISTINCTIVE THING ABOUT ANDRII'S CAR the morning I met him by the side of the road in Kupyansk, eastern Ukraine, was that it was full of pastries; the backseat was piled high with bagels and biscuits.

In contrast, the front seats were covered in flak jackets, which felt unnerving and out of place. The juxtaposition of these two sets of things made no sense at all, until Andrii told me his role in the war. He greeted me with a big smile under his helmet. He talked energetically about the artillery unit we were going to visit, taking valuable supplies. He said, "They were fine about you coming because you are drawing and not taking photos. They are interested to see what you will draw."

Although I never felt that Andrii forgot I was a reporter, our conversation that morning ranged widely. We talked about his wife, who had returned to Kharkiv from Poland, fearing that they might split up if they weren't together. They had a son, Ivan, age eight. Like many children in Ukraine, Ivan was at school online.

Andrii told me, "My wife gets jealous because I speak with the guys all the time. I feel the fighters in this unit are like my children. I come here three times a week and bring them food and medicine. I also take their laundry away. It's difficult now for my family, because I am volunteering a lot. My wife is fine with it, but I don't bring any money home. It's not easy. If she and Ivan weren't here, I would go to Bakhmut. She supports me but the everyday questions are difficult to resolve."

We chatted about his volunteering and his work for the next hour, as we drove along the road from Kupyansk, south-east towards Luhansk and the frontline. The road was bumpy and muddy but not empty, and we passed several civilian cars marked with a white cross to denote Ukrainian military use. As we neared the frontline, we passed a sign spray-painted in Russian: "Добро пожаловать вад". Translated it means "Welcome to hell", a message left by the Ukrainians all across the country as a greeting to the invading Russian forces.

DMYTRO, 37

Commander, wounded soldier

KYIV

WHEN I MET DMYTRO IN A BAR in north-east Kyiv, he was waiting for his wife and drinking a Long Island Iced Tea. I could see a few scars poking out of the bottom of his sleeve on his left arm, but other than that Dmytro looked largely unscathed. This was surprising, because I had come to interview him as the soldier who had been shot twenty times by Russian machine guns in an ambush in Kharkiv Oblast, a year earlier.

Dmytro tells his story . . .

It happened in a district of Kharkiv, in a place called Pytomnyk, on May 11, 2022. We have had many losses in Pytomnyk—it is not a good position for either defense or attack. I was only there for one day.

I am the commander of an anti-aircraft and air defense unit. The job of the unit is to protect us from drones, rockets, and helicopters. I have a team of twenty people under me, of whom maybe six are young men.

On May 11, I got instructions to change my position. I took four people and a truck. We took all our clothes and our rockets with us. I said to the boys, "I will drive with the driver and you should follow in your vehicle 200 yards behind." We came to a village with very narrow streets. Once in the village we took a turning and came face-to-face with five Russians. They were regular soldiers and they were fifteen or twenty yards in front of us! They had two machine guns—how do you say? Called PKM? Three of the soldiers had typical AKs.

". . . I don't want to die in a burning car."

Our vehicle stopped. I thought about what I needed to do . . . I knew I should try to shoot them . . . and this thought took maybe three or four seconds. Then after that they started shooting us. This continued for about ten seconds. I didn't have time to shoot . . .

I spun round and two bullets went into my body, one through the ribs close to my heart, and the other near my stomach. The other bullets hit my legs, head, neck, and left arm. My right hand was the only bit that wasn't hit.

After about twenty seconds I saw that my bags and clothes were on fire. I thought maybe I'm going to die today, but I don't want to die in a burning car.

I had four Stinger missiles in the back of the truck, and I knew that if they exploded there wouldn't be anything of me left. I opened the truck door and fell onto the street. I tried to . . . how do you say—not walk—crawl, as I only had my hand and right leg on the floor. I saw my comrade Yarik, he wasn't moving on the other side of the vehicle. He was only twenty years old. Sadly he died—the only man from my squad who didn't make it.

First of all I sent a message on the radio to other people in the area about the five Russians. Then I called my guys in the car behind. Serhii came to me and I told him what to do. We used three tourniquets. I tried to put on one tourniquet but I couldn't. It wasn't the pain, but I couldn't do it with just one hand.

I never lost consciousness. From the moment I was shot to when I got to the surgeon's table, I kept my mind.

I gave orders to Serhii. I told him to put the tourniquet there, there, and there. **[Dmytro points to his left arm and both legs.]** I tried to touch my eyes and chin but Serhii pushed my hands away. He said, "Don't touch that. You have injuries everywhere and you have dirty hands." My eye hasn't seen since that day.

Julia, my wife, is an English teacher. Which is a shame for me because I know that my English is not very good! Sometimes at night she takes the phone, when there is no electricity in Kyiv, and she shines the light in my eye. She says my eye looks like the Terminator. When this is over, I would very much like to have children.

I was in hospital for three months and two weeks, which at that time was more than I had been in the war! First hospital in Kharkiv, then Poltava, then Kyiv, followed by six months of rehabilitation. Then I had more surgery on my leg, and then some rehabilitation.

These days I go regularly to the hospital, to see a specialist to check my bones, my eyes, and my injuries, and to see whether I can go back to the army or not. I am hoping I will be ready to go back in two or three months. The army will decide whether I can or whether I am out. But I am assuming I won't be able to go back because my physical situation isn't good. My left hand is . . . awful. Also, my leg . . . I have these things . . . orthotics! Without them my foot would . . . **[He stops talking and flops his wrist over, to explain that his foot would hang down and drag along the floor.]**

My body needs time to fix itself but like this, today I am not good for my country. I tried to change my work in the army to work with computers, but unfortunately

"My eye hasn't seen since that day."

the army doesn't need that type of work, so I decided to go back to my last job as a test engineer. I have a wife and one hand; I can work.

I have had eighteen operations—the last one was last November and I think I will need two more on my knee. One will be an easy operation and the other one not so easy. Our doctors don't want to do the difficult one in Ukraine, so perhaps I will go to Europe. One night Julia and I tried to work out how many scars I have and we counted 32 scars—twenty bullet holes in total.

". . . we counted 32 scars— twenty bullet holes in total."

After the first surgery, which took twenty hours, I took a photo of the number of packets of blood they gave me. It was eleven packs in all. I weighed 180 lbs before the injuries, and one month afterwards I weighed 145 lbs. And when the medical orderlies woke me up that day they said, "Good morning, lucky boy . . . you are very well. You have many bullet injuries." And they showed me the packet of bullets. "All of your body was covered in so many scars and bullets and do you know . . . ?" I didn't know what they were talking about . . . "And . . . your penis too . . ." And I thought, no . . . . what did you say about my penis? I wondered what I would say to my wife . . . I was very scared, I couldn't believe it. I had to check immediately. They weren't joking! I had been hit in my penis too! Luckily it has recovered from its small injury!

[Dmytro shows me his tattoos.]

This one, "Remember who you are," is one I had the first time I went into the army in 2014. When I hold a weapon in my hands it just reminds me to have a clear mind and not do anything bad. Many people who take weapons for the first time think they are like a god and that they can do anything they want.

I think everything will be alright in the end, but I know this war will continue for a long time. It is difficult for Ukrainian people.

Yesterday, March 9, was the birthday of the poet Taras Shevchenko. The Russians reminded us that they are terrorists—about 81 rockets fell yesterday.

It's funny . . . after the operation on my left hand, it was very swollen and the nerves were damaged so my hand went floppy. I tried physiotherapy but it didn't seem to work. Then I had a dream about this computer game called "Redemption Two," which I've always liked but have never played. I set it up on my computer and tried to click the buttons, with no success. I kept playing and after two weeks my hand started working properly again. Look—it's pretty good from playing every day, although it feels a bit numb. But if you saw it two months ago you would be impressed, as it was in a very bad, bad situation.

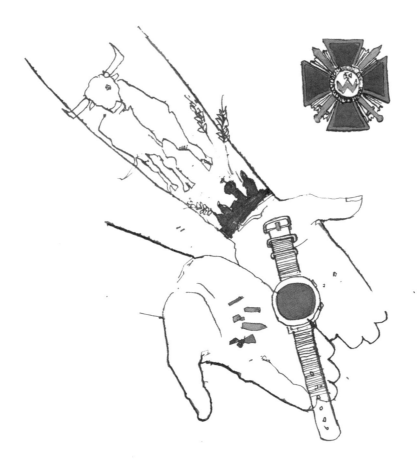

☐ **Dmytro's tattoos and the shrapnel removed from his body,** *Kyiv, March 10, 2023*

МУЗЕЙ
МЕДУЗ

ARTEM, 40

Jellyfish keeper

KYIV

I MET ARTEM IN AN UNDERGROUND half-lit room. He had a serious look on his face and a wet-shaved head, and was wearing a dark tracksuit. But this was not a bunker on the frontline in Donbas, nor were we in the bomb shelters of Bucha or Kherson. Artem was showing me the Jellyfish Museum on Kyiv's main street, just next to McDonald's, where he was like a father to these strange sea creatures.

He appeared a warm, openly emotional man, and I found myself listening intently when he smiled and told me about his work. Artem was responsible for the museum and, against all the odds, he was determined to keep this seemingly unimportant tourist attraction open in the middle of a war.

He started telling me his story as we stood in the pitch dark, surrounded by minute, delicate, bright-pink jellyfish that rotated slowly in the turquoise water of their tanks. Artem was shy at first, and, like so many Ukrainians, exhausted after one year of war. He wasn't sure whether talking to journalists was worthwhile. But his politeness won out and we began.

Artem tells his story . . .

After Maidan [the revolution in 2014] it was difficult, emotionally, to set up a restaurant here, in this place [Khreshchatyk Street]. People had died in the square and were scarred by all the shootings that had taken place. Working at a museum seemed more appropriate. Years before, I had seen a jellyfish museum in Japan, so I tried to set up one here in Kyiv. The museum is now four years old and we have collected eighteen species. It's been a hard thing to start, especially in Ukraine, but we learn and we keep trying.

On February 24, 2022, after the invasion, of course we didn't come to work. On the 25th I went to the military office to volunteer as a soldier and asked them if they needed me. They said that they didn't, so I took a bicycle and went to the museum. The jellyfish need to be fed every day, three times a day, otherwise they become small and die. At that time, the road was blocked by the military, and I wasn't allowed to go into the museum. I went home, and as I live on the 21st floor of a block of apartments in the north-east of Kyiv, I could see we were being surrounded by Russians.

On February 26 one of my friends called me from an area south of the city, which was not surrounded by Russian soldiers. I decided to move my family to his house in Rzhyshchiv. Then I joined the Territorial Defense Force [civilian volunteers who are used as military reserves] and I started working at a checkpoint in the area. I didn't come back to Kyiv until March 5, when I returned to the museum. Some of the tanks had been disconnected from the electricity and although some of the jellyfish were still alive, about 25% had died.

Once again the military told me I shouldn't be here, so I decided to switch off all the electricity, because there was a fire risk, and in doing so, I let all the jellyfish die. It was very moving for me, because I nurtured them from the beginning. It was emotional because . . . of course . . . jellyfish don't have brains as such, but when you care for them, you love them all.

". . . jellyfish don't have brains as such, but when you care for them, you love them all."

"... the museum is one of the few places in modern Ukraine that allows people, albeit briefly, to escape from the war ..."

It was hard for me to leave, but I took a tank with the jellyfish polyps I had collected before the war with me and sent this box to my friends in Lviv, in the hope that they might be able to save them. But the delivery service took fourteen days to get to Lviv instead of one day, and most of the polyps died.

At the end of March 2022 I came back to Kyiv, and I returned to the museum. The dangers around Kyiv had lessened and I began to think about what to do next. I believe that the museum is one of the few places in modern Ukraine that allows people, albeit briefly, to escape from the war and the ongoing turmoil and change around us. It is a very peaceful place where you can forget everything and enjoy creatures that, in spite of everything, have existed on our land for more than 500,000,000 years. The jellyfish inspire us with their example of survival.

[When Artem came back to Kyiv in March 2022, he arranged for new polyps to be sent from Spain. Once again the electricity was cut in April for two weeks, and once again they had to start from scratch. The museum opened briefly on August 15 but blackouts started in October, and 60% of the jellyfish died. Now, a year later, life in Ukraine is no more certain, but the museum is open to visitors, and attracts many of them despite the war.]

I have one son and one daughter, aged nineteen and ten years old. They are living with their mother in a little town just outside Dublin, in Ireland. I will get to see them when they come back to Kyiv soon. My wife and I have a joke that she is very beautiful but my jellyfish are in competition with her!

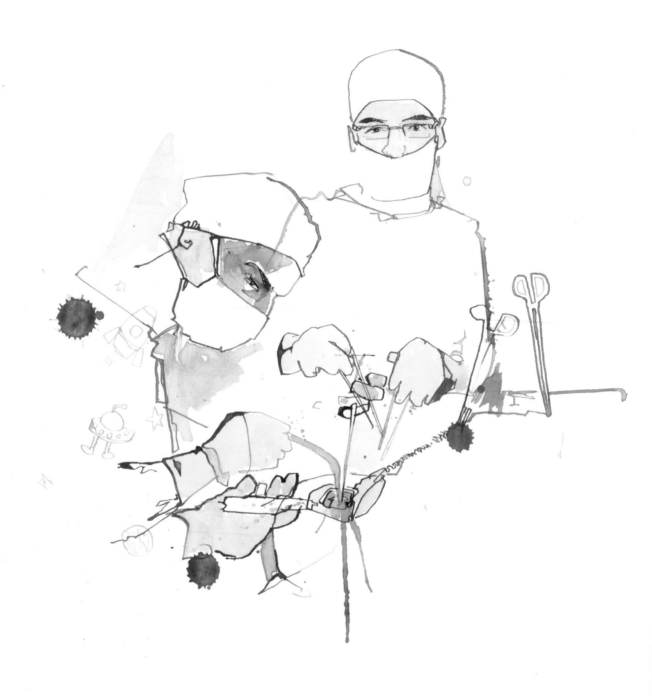

DR. KYRYLO & DR. OLEKSANDR

Father & son, neurosurgeons

KHARKIV

YOU WOULD THINK THAT THE NUMBER OF BEDS in Ukrainian hospital corridors was a good indicator of the level of atrocities unfolding in the country. It certainly looked this way in Kharkiv City Clinical Hospital. But in fact these beds were not here because the hospital was busy—far from it. Most of the population in the east of Ukraine had moved away or moved abroad. The patients were there because the few who were left preferred to sleep in the corridors, one more concrete wall away from the bomb blasts on the other side of the cellophane-taped windows.

Denys, a patient, was surrounded by some of Ukraine's greatest medical minds, who were, at that moment, drilling into his skull. Dr. Kyrylo was removing a 2-inch piece of skull from above Denys's right ear so that he could get to, and extract, the haematoma below. Dr. Oleksandr, Dr. Kyrylo's father, was watching and joked, "It's family business," before he quickly began listing the patients they were operating on next.

There was electricity, there was clean medical equipment, and the hour-long operation was a success. There was nothing unusual about carrying out this sophisticated operation in Ukraine at this time—the doctors continued to work as normally as possible. The context in which this team carried out this work was anything but normal, though, as all around them a war raged, the likes of which hadn't been seen in Europe since 1945.

Dr. Kyrylo tells his story . . .

This is a city of courageous glory, of strong and brave people—my dear city of Kharkiv. To be honest, we have been doing the same work as I have always done—since I started doing neurosurgery. This is ordinary work—a daily routine, except that outside, bombs were falling. Since February 2023, I was honored to be chief of the pediatric neurosurgical department in our hospital. This is the department that my dad headed before then. He is chief now for adult patients. Certainly in those moments in time of war, being alone would have been easier than working together!

The beginning of hostilities and war was for everyone a huge stress, full of fear and a lack of understanding of what to do. Since I worked as a neurosurgeon in an emergency hospital, I decided that I would stay in my clinic and help the wounded, as well as provide care to the general population of adults and children. When the war started, I took my family abroad to Slovakia. At the time, I could not imagine that we would not see each other for a whole year. My wife was then seven months pregnant and my little daughter was four years old.

"It was very scary to operate on patients when bombs were falling . . ."

It was very scary to operate on patients when bombs were falling and exploding around us. It was difficult to focus. At the same time, the entire neurosurgical team understood that we couldn't stop or pause an operation in the middle and pick it up again after, say, half an hour, when the shelling had stopped. Therefore, we all tried to make light of what was happening, to detach ourselves from it. For example, we constantly said that the sounds of explosions were outgoing rockets, not real rocket explosions on the ground.

Not much has changed in the hospital since last year. There are more doctors and medical personnel, as many have returned from abroad. Now there are fewer explosions, but still they happen.

I remember several experiences through this difficult period that stand out. There was one person who we operated on during a very strong shelling. We had a very severe bleeding in the wound, and we could not stop it for a long time. All this time, the shelling

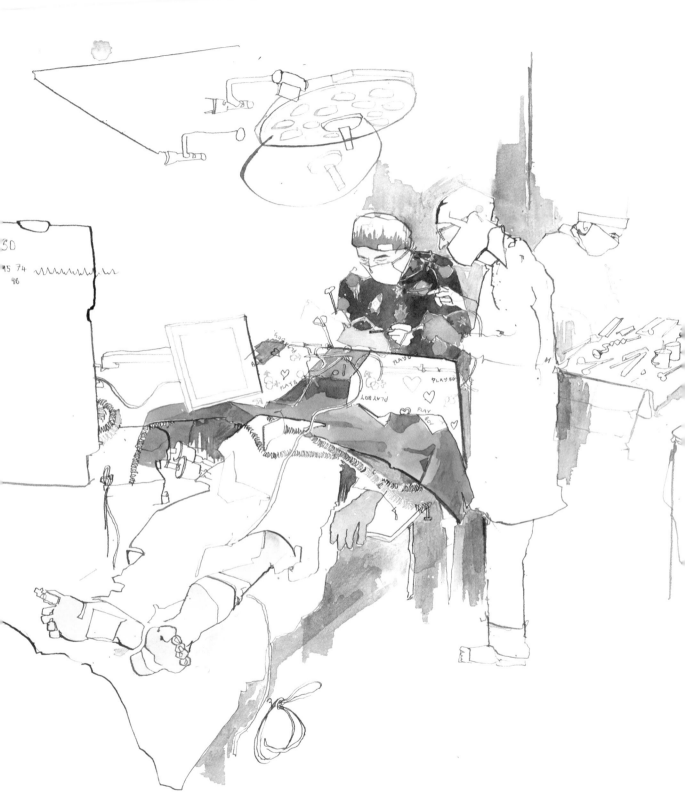

☐ **Denys undergoes neurosurgery to remove a blood clot,** *Kharkiv, March 30, 2022*

continued. In the end we managed to stop it and the patient recovered and was discharged home. There was another patient who was crushed when a door fell on her while she was at home, during an airstrike. She had an open craniocerebral injury, after which she had to undergo plastic surgery and we gave her an artificial eye.

There were other times when we had power outages and we were forced to operate under extremely difficult conditions. For example, one time we brought the patient into the operating theatre and then the electricity was completely turned off. We had to quickly take the patient to another operating theatre, where there was a generator. We owe a lot to our chief doctor and the leaders of the city authorities who helped us stay afloat. We are also very grateful to our colleagues and charities abroad who have sent us all kinds of surgical assistance. It has helped us a lot.

I have no message or word for the inhabitants of our hostile neighboring state to the east, who have brought us grief, blood, and death.

I believe and hope that we will soon win this war and finally peace will come to our wonderful, united country, and we will begin to restore everything that was destroyed.

". . . we will begin to restore everything that was destroyed."

TATIANA, 17

Patient

KHARKIV

ONE OF DR. OLEKSANDR'S PATIENTS WAS TATIANA. She lay in her hospital bed and looked at me with only one eye. The other, sadly, will never open again.

Tatiana lost her eye when she was caught in an explosion in Kharkiv region in March 2022. Her head was shaved after the operation and I could clearly see the scar that ran from her forehead down through the middle of her eye socket to her cheekbone. Her smile showed off her beauty though and it lit up the whole of her face, transcending the disfiguration of one side, something that should have no place on someone so young.

ANATOLII, 48

Mechanic, father

KHARKIV

IN A SECRET FACILITY ON THE OUTSKIRTS OF KHARKIV, while Ukrainian Armed Forces waited for new tanks to arrive from Germany, America, and the United Kingdom, Anatolii, Ivan, and Serhii worked tirelessly to fix broken tanks and armored personnel carriers (APCs), to bolster the Ukrainian war effort. Some of the vehicles were Ukrainian, but others were Russian, captured, repurposed, and sent back to the frontline. Two of the Russian tanks in this colossal facility had already been back to the frontline more than once. Others lay in a heap, with the infamous Russian "Z" sign sprayed all over them, waiting to be used for spare parts or scrapped.

This complex of giant workshops belonging to the 14th Mechanized Brigade was the size of several football fields. Its location was kept secret by ensuring only a very low flow of traffic around where it was hidden among the sprawling light industrial complexes from the Soviet era that make up part of Kharkiv. Hidden in plain sight, Anatolii and his team finished at four o'clock each day so that no lights would attract unwanted attention. The warehouses were linked by internal doors, so that workers wouldn't be seen outside in military uniform. Photographs of the buildings, the skyline, or the roof were strictly forbidden.

I watched Anatolii work, standing on a broken stepladder with a welding iron, a box of wrenches, and a head lamp. He'd use anything to get these vehicles working again and back on the frontline. Many of them had roughly sprayed white crosses or painted yellow barrels, so that they could be identified by their own infantry.

While the headline news topics were about nuclear escalation and technical weaponry, the reality of the war on the ground was shown by these hard-working Ukrainian people, and scenes like these, unchanged from the past.

Interviewed March 19, 2023

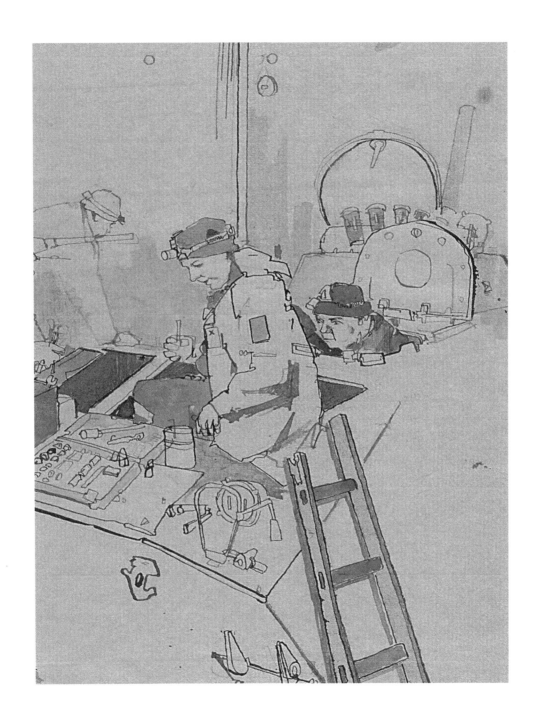

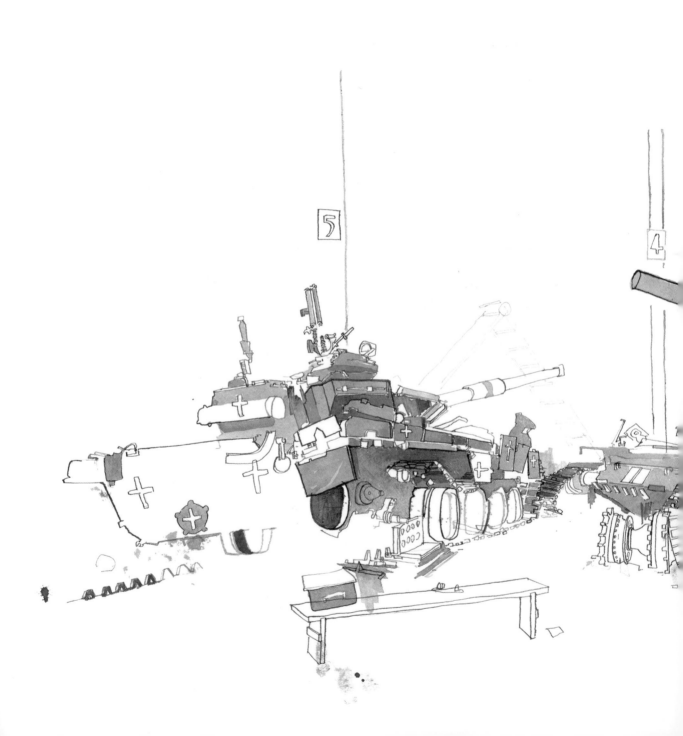

Anatolii tells his story . . .

I am the chief mechanic. I have worked at this for 30 years. They say I have golden hands, because I have repaired most of the Ukrainian military equipment and tanks here. This last year has been increasingly difficult. Sometimes there is nothing to repair—the explosions completely destroy everything. Every day we do the same thing. The worst part of this job for me is to always have dirty hands and dirty clothes, but the hope of victory gives me hope and energy to move on and continue with my job.

☐ **14th Mechanized Brigade warehouse,** *Kharkiv, March 19, 2023*

☐ **14th Mechanized Brigade mending APCs,** *Kharkiv, March 19, 2023*

SERHII, 58

Architect

KHARKIV

SERHII AND I MET IN THE CORRIDOR OF A HOSPITAL IN KHARKIV. He was different from many of the other patients in the hospital. He was cheerful and moved around the ward on his crutches, chatting. He had a bandage wrapped around his head. I asked the nurse what had happened to him and she told me, "He says his house fell on his head." And as she said this Serhii grinned, as if to make light of it all. In fact almost everything Serhii said was delivered with a smile—unusual in Ukraine at the time. When I asked if I could draw him, he said only if he could draw me, too. In sign language and broken English, we arranged to meet the following day.

By the time I arrived in the empty ward room, Serhii was in position on one of the beds, and he got up to present me proudly with a drawing he had made overnight. It was in pencil on a piece of cardboard. It showed a Russian tank with a swastika on it, driving towards a little girl waving a Ukrainian flag. An apt caricature of life in Kharkiv at the time, he thought.

We drew each other and Serhii grinned self-deprecatingly and made excuses about his pencils not being very good. We swapped drawings and stayed in touch. Several months later I was able to ask him some questions.

This interview is made up from several emails from Serhii, who had to use a friend's computer. One of Serhii's passionate suggestions was to use a lower case "r" instead of a capital letter for the Russians. I'm sorry, Serhii, I haven't done that throughout the whole book.

Serhii tells his story . . .

I, Serhii, was born in 1964. 58 years old. I remember everything from my childhood very well. I was born and raised in the city of Kharkiv, in the house of my grandfather, which this ill-fated russian rocket hit . . .

The USSR is eighteen years of my life. In those days we lived and believed in a bright future, which our state promised us. Ukraine and our city of Kharkiv lived quite well—not as much as the whole of civilized Europe, of course, but we did not live in poverty. There was a certain stability, good wages, development prospects, and of course no one could imagine what would happen in the new millennium. Such a terrible change . . .

The story of that day, March 16, 2022, will remain in my memory forever. . . . It was the evening, I'm sitting with my dog, drinking tea, suddenly *bang-bang-bang-bang*, the fifth *bang* hit my house. I remember only the whistle and the beginning of the explosion. I woke up fifteen minutes later. The rocket exploded three yards away from me, in the bedroom. My dog and I were bombarded with bricks from the walls. Somehow we got out, the rescuers helped to dig us out. Well . . . then the ambulance came, I went to the No. 4 Emergency Hospital. I had skull surgery, rehabilitation followed, and all that . . .

I am very grateful to all the doctors and friends for their help, God bless them!

Our Kharkiv has already moved a little away from that sudden and terrible shock of February 2022. Gradually the city comes to life, people return from other countries to their apartments and houses. I am restoring my house little by little. There is still a lot of work after the explosion. I take care of my small home garden—recently I went to the suburbs for porcini mushrooms!

And of course, I draw again, I paint small oil paintings.

We will restore everything that is destroyed! And it will be even better than it was before the war! Putin will soon die and there will be a real world, the Ukrainian WORLD! We have a future, they don't!

We dream of peace, freedom, and the joy of being without war.

"I remember only the whistle and the beginning of the explosion."

Sometimes I go to my friend Alexander—he lives not far from me, near the Kharkiv River, which flows through our city. We communicate, fish, listen to music, and enjoy nature, temporarily forgetting about war, sorrows and sorrows. And only the explosions of russian missiles and the howl of sirens do not allow you to completely relax.

I think that it is useless to re-educate the russians (with a small "r"). You just need to remove, destroy, erase them from our Ukrainian land, judge Putin and his gang by the highest mortal court! As long as they are alive, there will be no peace anywhere!

My opinion is only death to russian fascists! Damn them! The russians are already morally broken and almost lost the war, and Ukraine has become much stronger during this time, thanks to its allies and friends! And russia (with a small letter) is waiting for retribution, for evil and meanness, because the Lord God always punishes aggressors and rapists!

We strongly believe in the victory of Ukraine and in the Supreme Court over the russian fascists!

I'm sorry for such direct and sharp statements. It boiled, it's already deep inside, deep in my soul . . .

"We dream of peace, freedom, and the joy of being without war."

TYMUR, 18

Music student, translator

LONDON

TYMUR ARRIVED IN LONDON IN APRIL 2022 with his sister Karina. He left his father and brother behind in Kyiv and his mother in Warsaw. Each week he took part in a peaceful protest opposite Downing Street, to remind UK politicians that Ukraine must not be forgotten.

I met his family in Kyiv. His father, Nadir, was born in Afghanistan and was sent to the Soviet Union to study as a top music student. There he met Svitlana, a singer, and they got married and had three children. Nadir had eleven brothers and sisters. All were still in Afghanistan, except for one sister who came to Ukraine to escape the Taliban, but found herself fleeing to Poland shortly after the war started.

I spoke to Tymur in London, where he now lived with a host family while he finished his A-levels. He was working as a translator in Norfolk with the Ministry of Defense, in support of Ukrainian soldiers.

Tymur tells his story . . .

I was at home in northern Kyiv with my mom and my brother. My father was working in the countryside. I read the news at 11 p.m. on February 23, 2022. The rising tension began with President Zelensky appealing to the world for help.

It was obvious that the situation wasn't good! At 2 a.m. I started preparing supplies of water and food in case we needed to run away, and put them in a backpack. I was so tired by 3 a.m. I fell asleep, even though I knew what was about to happen. At 5 a.m. I woke to the sounds of explosions and my mom running around the apartment screaming, "They are bombing us, they are bombing us." Within ten minutes my father came and we evacuated to the countryside.

I didn't feel any emotion. I tried to keep my mind cool but I tried to prepare myself for any outcome.

We had to take my father's sister and her family with us, too. In 2020 they had come from Afghanistan. They were fleeing the Taliban and they were trying to settle in Kyiv. There were fourteen of us in all to start with. We stayed in the countryside for a week. But within the first three days our Afghan relatives left for Poland. My father drove them to the railway station. We were really scared for him because at the time it was still incredibly dangerous to go to the center of Kyiv.

"We made Molotov cocktails in the garage . . ."

We just ate bread for the first three days—that is all we had. We were expecting the Russians to come and we made Molotov cocktails in the garage . . .

There was one really intense situation when I thought we were going to die. My brother, father, and sister's husband had all left to get some gasoline. My sister rushed downstairs and told me that she had seen someone with an AK-47 right beside our house. We thought it might be a looter, or a soldier. I tried to stay calm, and I told everyone to get out of the room while I looked. I peeped at him through a tiny gap in the window. I couldn't see which color stripe he had on his arm to indicate whether he was Russian or Ukrainian. The Russians and the Ukrainians wear almost the same uniform. I had to remain calm.

I made sure that everyone had a weapon—to increase their chances of survival. But my sister was hysterical and she was panicking. Tense moments passed, but finally we realized the soldier was one of ours.

It was funny to sleep in the countryside after that—we were civilians with weapons. My sister's husband had this pneumatic pistol, my uncle had a pistol with rubber bullets, and I had a knife and a tomahawk. And every night I would put the tomahawk underneath my pillow, and I didn't even have a proper belt, but I just tied the knife around my waist.

Surprisingly I still slept. I thought that we had to have someone on night watch, so I stayed up late, until I fell asleep exhausted. During this period, I lost track of time. It passed so slowly. It was a nightmare, two weeks felt like five years at a time. And now a year later it feels like just one moment.

It's this feeling of the war that has inspired one of my music tracks. It's a feeling of anxiety—it's all anxiety. It's meant to sound hyper-tense. I like the way it feels really, really long and repetitive. That is the main feeling that I have when we are waiting.

"This was one of the countless horrors of war."

Eventually when it was safer, my dad and brother went back to Kyiv. I was allowed to leave the country under martial law. My group included all the women and me. I was seventeen.

We left Ukraine on March 12. The next day we found a car and paid them to take us to the border, and we crossed the border by foot. There weren't any problems. There was a guy in a wheelchair who was disabled but he didn't have his papers so they wouldn't let him cross for a long time, and there was a woman being really highly stressed by this. It felt really hard to see. This was one of the countless horrors of war.

Then we took a bus to Warsaw and stayed there for about a month. It was a strange feeling to be safe. Human beings adapt to everything really quickly, and I felt really strange. I had already adapted to war.

□ **Protests outside Downing Street,** *London, January 21, 2023*

On April 30 I came to England with my sister, Karina. We arrived as refugees, we had our passports with an email from the Home Office and a letter from my sponsor, Louise.

In London it feels really important to me to be part of something Ukrainian. I believe the demonstrations [outside Downing Street] are effective for Ukrainians living here. It's important to show people that we care and that it's not a war that is just happening in Ukraine, but it is a war that is happening around the world. And it's the war of democracy against totalitarianism. Then we can unite against evil and can unite around something greater than just ourselves.

I have been working as a translator in a military camp in the UK, training Ukrainian soldiers. They are newbies and they have never held a weapon before. Yesterday they were civilians and today they have come to train to fight the Russians.

"I feel like I owe a lot to Ukraine."

I will go back to the camp for another five weeks and I receive my A-level results on August 17. I have actually forgotten about them. When I said goodbye to the Ukrainian guys that are in training, it just feels like there are much more important things in my life than A-levels. I'm not sure what those guys will be doing but I know that they are in Ukraine right now.

If I get into university I will start in September, but first I will see my mother. She is coming to England for a month. I just really want to see her before she goes back to Ukraine. It is going to be moving to see her. I last saw her six months ago. She is called Svitlana and "svitlo" means light. For me she is like the sun, she is really vibrant.

I feel drawn back to Ukraine. All the things that are happening to me now are thanks to Ukraine, NOT because of Ukraine. And I feel like I have a lot to pay back to one of my homelands. I don't think Afghanistan gave me that much, as I didn't grow up there. But I grew up in Ukraine so I feel lots of . . . I feel like I owe a lot to Ukraine.

If I think about the war too much then it starts to scare me. I try not to think that much about my family, and when I start, I can't hold my tears back, so I prefer not to.

I don't see an end to this. However depressing that sounds. It's hard to say but it is much harder to think about. There won't be a peaceful treaty.

STOP

STOP GENOCIDE

UKRAINIAN KIDS ARE PRO-TECTING YOU FROM MISSILE

THANK YOUR SU

ZAP

Ленин
Сталин

☐ **Protests outside Downing Street,** *London, January 21, 2023*

LARYSA

Headmistress

SALTIVKA, KHARKIV

LARYSA STAYED BEHIND IN THE SCHOOL she was headmistress of in North Saltivka, to provide shelter for the local residents who had fled their homes or felt unsafe in them under heavy Russian bombardment. All of the staff had left, but, supported by her husband and son, she saw this as her duty to the community. Despite the gymnasium being shelled, several families lived in the basement of the school. Saltivka was hit by heavy and indiscriminate Russian artillery for weeks on end. Days after I visited, the school was evacuated when another missile struck.

Interviewed April 4, 2022 & August 8, 2023

Larysa tells her story . . .

We all believed that the war was someone's mistake and everything would end quickly. We understood that people needed help to survive this situation. Among the people who stayed were my own parents and grandchildren. I have been at this school since 1971, from the day it was established—first as a student, then as a laboratory assistant, then as a primary school teacher, deputy director—almost my whole life was connected with the school. Everything was familiar here: walls, people, students, parents. That's why, together with my husband and son, I decided to stay in Kharkiv at the school.

On February 24, 2022, at 5 a.m., we were woken up by inexplicable roars, alarms, and rumblings. Social networks announced the beginning of a military invasion by the Russian Federation. It was unexpected for us, ordinary people. We could not believe what was happening. The suspension of the educational process was announced immediately. Those teachers who lived next to the school came to work that day; they put their papers in order and reassured people (both adults and children) who had already arrived at the school that morning and were now sheltering in the basement—a shooting range.

From then on my family did not leave the school until June 1, 2022. We stayed there around the clock while there were people living in the basement. Later when teachers, technicians, and guards began to return, we stayed in the building only during the day. We went home to spend the night in our house, which was located nearby.

It became especially difficult in our area (North Saltivka) from March 3, 2022, when the first shelling of schools, houses, and kindergartens began. At that time, there were more than 200 people (children, mothers, grandmothers, grandfathers) in the basement. After the first shelling, people were frightened and started leaving

". . . people were frightened and started leaving to save their loved ones."

to save their loved ones. And on March 3, 2022, I was the only employee left at the school. There was no light for nine days. Gas pipes were broken in some houses. Everyone mucked in and helped: somebody cooked food and ran home with it, somebody looked for water, somebody found where to charge cell phones (there was no communication, no internet). The first volunteers appeared and started bringing water, food and medicine.

From March 9, 2022, we started giving out food to residents of the area who did not live in the school building. We fed more than 300 people a day. Food was cooked in kindergarten No. 80, and my family and a group of volunteers who were living in the school distributed food. There were very few people left in the neighborhood. It seemed that life had stopped. There was either a terrible silence or frequent shelling noises. Everyone was afraid to come to our area. Everything—shops and clinics—were all closed. We could only help each other with what we had. Medicines were ordered through volunteers. It was amazing that primary school teachers who stayed in Kharkiv, school graduates, parents of students, all risked their lives to come and bring everything we needed: water, medicine, food. Everyone who was in our area became one big family.

People of different ages and families lived in the basement. They needed to adapt to each other, learn to find a common language. It was not easy. In order to maintain the state of health, to comply with sanitary standards, cleaning shifts were arranged. It was difficult to adjust to the darkness when there was no light, the flashlights were running out of batteries. Another problem was, when the heating was turned off after the shelling, it started to feel damp and cool, especially as the sleeping places were on the floor.

"It seemed that life had stopped."

In May 2022 all the families who lived with us either returned home or were allocated to a dormitory (if their housing had been destroyed). Some went abroad or to other regions of Ukraine. They are safe now.

There were particular problems with the school when the windows, roof, heating system, sports hall, and doors were damaged. The wall of the first floor, which was adjacent to the shelter, was destroyed, leading to cold, dampness, and danger for people. At first, the windows and the wall were fixed with any materials we could find, until volunteers helped and an additional exit was created in the basement. It calmed people down, gave them hope for survival.

Today, the school is functioning: the destroyed wall, the walls of the first floor, and the heating system have been restored and the windows are boarded up with chipboard. The shelter was painted and whitewashed, the floor was tiled, the walls were sheathed, the ventilation was repaired, and the lighting was renovated. There are flower gardens and lawns in the school grounds. People who live in the neighborhood spend their free time on the sports grounds of the school. The educational process has been resumed online since April 12, 2022. The total number of classes is 32: there are 885 students in them. Students successfully study, participate and win promotions—these are volunteer movements, tournaments, Olympiads, contests, and competitions.

We have always believed that we are a part of Ukraine. Like every Ukrainian, we believe in and hope for victory, peace, restoration of Ukraine, Kharkiv, and our school. We are a strong nation.

"Like every Ukrainian, we believe in and hope for victory, peace, restoration of Ukraine . . ."

НАВЧАЛЬНЕ
МІСЦЕ №2

□ **Basement living in Kharkiv School No 141,** *Saltivka, Kharkiv, April 4, 2022*

ILLIA, 4

Brother

KUPYANSK

"WE CALL HIM THE BALLERINA because his legs point outwards," Illia said to me, pointing to a small scruffy dog standing next to him.

I met Illia, aged four, and his older brother Andrii outside their mother's shawarma and pizza shop, in Kupyansk. Inside was a hive of activity, and the boys could come and go through the swing door, playing outside despite the distant rumbles of war. The boys were known in the street and everyone who lived there kept an eye out for them.

Watching them play gave me a sense of what childhood in Ukraine was like at that moment. While Illia ate two enormous sticky buns out of a packet, he assisted Andrii in digging a tiny grave with a lollipop stick, and burying a small plastic skeleton in the ground. The lollipop stick marked the grave so they could find it later, and they continued their game elsewhere in the street. They were followed closely by the odd-looking mongrel that Illia had amusingly called the Ballerina.

I often think about Illia and Andrii now and wonder where they are and what they are doing. I wonder what the world will be like and how it will change over their lifespan, and what will happen in their war-torn future.

Interviewed March 15, 2023

AFTERWORD

IT'S ALL TOO EASY TO FORGET that the stories in this book are unfolding in Ukraine, on the frontline, in the trenches, the hospitals and damaged homes as I write. I think about this all the time. Where are they all now? With the exception of Madame Olga (who was 99 when we met), all the subjects in this book are, at the time of writing, still alive. Olga died peacefully in her bed several months after I drew her. This book is dedicated to all the ordinary lives that had war delivered upon them.

As all these characters spoke to me, I learnt that their voices were of equal importance to the drawings. The drawing was a handshake but the words were delicate and moving, conveying lifetimes of experience. The act of drawing can be a solitary occupation, but the gathering of stories in a different language, at a vulnerable time, is a sensitive and empathetic process. I was in the hands of the Ukrainian fixers, translators, and drivers who helped me cross those barriers.

Often the Ukrainians I met didn't want to talk, because they didn't believe they had done anything heroic at all. Sometimes they spoke to me because they were bored, or kind, or because talking to a stranger was a chance to share the weight of their trauma without judgment. Sometimes people in trouble speak to the press not because they want to, but because they think it just might make a difference. Taking advantage of that was my greatest fear. I felt that drawing was a gentle way in. And it gave me a chance to sit and listen for longer—to provide an unthreatening alternative to the modern photo-journalist.

The saddest thing about interviewing people a year apart was that their problems and anxieties had in no way lessened. The grief was still tangible and the anguish still visible. They still had hopes and expectations for the future but these were becoming lost in the chaos. The only consolation for me was I could tell they felt relief knowing that others in the world knew what had happened to them and were horrified. In turn I felt relief in knowing that this will be literally in print for all to see. Although it is unlikely to make any difference to their individual situations.

Truth is an elusive objective in war reporting. It needs to be chased and checked and picked at. Ukraine could be the most documented war in history, but despite the brilliance of technology we still struggle to define what the "truth" is. The reality is that there are many "truths" within the turmoil.

The modern news industry is limited by the tools it has to tell the "truth." These drawings are a deliberately slow antidote to this limitation. They are not more or less true than a photograph or news report, but they are an important, first-hand account of the war that offers texture, longevity, and depth to a subject that even now, nearly two full years on, with the fighting rampant, has dropped off the front pages.

If Volodymyr, now age 8, lives until he is 99 like Madame Olga, he will live to the year 2115. Will he be telling the same tormented stories as Olga? Or can he hope for a better life? Interviewing people at different ends of their lives made me acutely aware of this circularity of war. We thought these scenes were committed to the history books. We were wrong.

George Butler, February 2024

ACKNOWLEDGMENTS

None of this work would have been possible without the assistance of the Ukrainians who have made it their mission to share what is happening in their country with the world, in the hope of support and change. I am grateful for their time and energy in finding the stories and keeping me safe.

Special thanks to . . .
Rita Burkovska, Max Burtsev, Roman Kriukov, Anna Lukinova, Mariana Matveichuk, Daria Mitiuk, Illia Novikov, Dzvinka Pinchuk, Volodymyr Roh, Ruslana, Dmytro Sharnin, Yevheniia Shevchuk, Lyzaveta Sokolova, Dmytro Tkachuk, Valentyna Vakulenko, and Liudmyla Yankina.

Thanks to . . .
Alexandra Bielikova, Edward Butler, Liam Chivers, Mick Clifford, Isabel Coles, Laurie Erlam, Ruth Ganesh, Martin Gray, Paul Grover, Molly Hunter, Mishal Husain, Gary Jones, Denise Johnstone-Burt, Campbell MacDiarmid, Oliver Marsden, Ben Norland, Philippa Perry, Paul Reyes, Tom Robinson, Quentin Sommerville, Birthe Steinbeck, Nghiem Ta, Kyle Thorburn, Lauren Van Metre, Susan Van Metre, Romilly Weeks, Jim Williams, and Zeeshan.

This work was supported by Pulitzer Center.

The publisher has made a donation to Superhumans Center in support of their work in providing prosthetics, reconstructive surgery, and rehabilitation to those injured in the conflict in Ukraine.

Superhumans Center is a modern clinic for prosthetics, rehabilitation, reconstructive surgery, and psychological support for military and civilians injured in the war in Ukraine. Superhumans is not a business. All services at the clinic are free for patients. The center is financed by donors and partners. The first Superhumans Center was opened in April, 2023 near Lviv (Ukraine). In the coming years, Superhumans will open five more centers in different cities of Ukraine: Kharkiv, Mykolaiv, Vinnytsia, Rivne, Dnipro. The project was initiated by Ukrainian businessman Andriy Stavnitser. You can learn more about Superhumans Center, and how to donate, at www.superhumans.com.

To find out more about the charity Legacy of War Foundation and their work in Ukraine, visit www.legacyofwarfoundation.com

☐ Magic Coffee Tram, run by Eliza, age 17, in amongst the tank traps,
Derybasivska Street, Odesa, March 16, 2022

ARTWORK NOTES

p. 1
Pen and hand

p. 2
**Independence Monument
wrapped in sandbags,**
Konstytutsii Square, Kharkiv
March 31, 2022
(23 $^5/_8$" x 16 $^9/_{16}$")

p. 4
**Odesa National Academic
Theatre of Opera and Ballet,**
Odesa
March 15, 2022
(16 $^9/_{16}$" x 23 $^5/_8$")

p. 6
Destroyed Russian convoy,
Vokzalna Street, Bucha
April 6, 2022
(23 $^5/_8$" x 16 $^9/_{16}$")

p. 16   **Madame Olga**

p. 20
**Lines before curfew at the
EKO Market,** *Kyiv*
March 21, 2022
(23 $^5/_8$" x 16 $^9/_{16}$")

p. 23
**Internally displaced people
waiting in Kyiv railway
station,** *Kyiv*
March 28, 2022
(11 $^{13}/_{16}$ x 16 $^9/_{16}$")

p. 24   **Petro**

p. 27
**Petro collecting books after a
missile strike,** *Kramatorsk*
March 14, 2023
(23 $^5/_8$" x 16 $^9/_{16}$")

p. 28
**Missile strike, near
Akademichna Street,**
Kramatorsk
March 14, 2023
(23 $^5/_8$" x 16 $^9/_{16}$")

p. 30   **Yurii**

p. 34
**A makeshift bridge under the
destroyed Irpin Bridge,**
Irpin, near Kyiv
April 7, 2022
(23 $^5/_8$" x 16 $^9/_{16}$")

p. 37   **Yara**

p. 40   **Mariia & Oleksandr**

p. 44
**Cement truck roadblock,
Soborna Street,** *Bucha*
April 6, 2022
(23 $^5/_8$" x 16 $^9/_{16}$")

p. 48
**Mass graves, St. Andrew's
Church,** *Bucha*
April 8, 2022
(23 $^5/_8$" x 16 $^9/_{16}$")

p. 50   **Dr. Yurii**

p. 54   **Volodymyr**

p. 58
**Kharkiv City Clinical
Hospital,** *Kharkiv*
March 29, 2022
(16 $^9/_{16}$" x 16 $^9/_{16}$")

p. 60   **Liza**

p. 65   **Serhii**

p. 65
**Sheltering underground,
Serpnia 23 Metro,** *Kharkiv*
April 1, 2022
(11 $^7/_{16}$" x 16 $^9/_{16}$")

p. 68
**Platform living – Lining up
for borscht, Serpnia 23 Metro,**
Kharkiv
March 31, 2022
(23 $^5/_8$" x 16 $^9/_{16}$")

p. 70
**Platform living, Serpnia 23
Metro,** *Kharkiv*
March 31, 2022
(23 $^5/_8$" x 16 $^9/_{16}$")

p. 72   **Anton**

p. 74
**Fixing an Mi-17 helicopter,
18th Separate Army Aviation
Brigade,** *Poltava*
March 20, 2023

p. 76   **Oleg**

p. 80
**Selling second hand things
at Rynok Starykh Rechey
Market,** *Kharkiv*
March 12, 2023

p. 83
**Night raids with Kharkiv
Police,** *Kharkiv*
April 3, 2022
(23 $^5/_8$" x 16 $^9/_{16}$")

p. 84   **Artem**

p. 96   **Andrii & Oleksandr**

These drawings are done
from life in ink, watercolor,
and collage. They were
done on A2 loose sheets.
Often they were colored in
afterwards to avoid being
somewhere dangerous for too
long. When the drawing got
in the way of the intimacy
of interview the portraits
you see were finished from
photographs afterwards.

This work was supported by the Pulitzer Center.

First US edition 2024

Library of Congress Catalog Card Number pending
ISBN 978-1-5362-4043-6

24 25 26 27 28 29 LGO 10 9 8 7 6 5 4 3 2

Printed in Vicenza, Italy

This book was typeset in Palatino.
The illustrations were done in ink, watercolor, and collage.

Candlewick Studio
an imprint of Candlewick Press
99 Dover Street, Somerville, Massachusetts 02144

www.candlewickstudio.com

These testimonies are the subjects' personal recollections of the war as recorded during interviews in situ, and have been edited only where necessary for clarity. The author is grateful to all the participants who agreed to have their names and portraits included in this book.
All statistics were accurate at the time of going to print.

☐ **Informal market stalls on Katerynyns'ka Street,** *Odesa*
· *March 15, 2022*